# On The M...
## Their Lies

# What Every Christian Needs To Know

MICHAEL W WITCOFF

Michael Witcoff

Copyright © 2018 Michael Witcoff

All rights reserved.

ISBN-13: 978-1986325479

ARMOR OF GOD MINISTRIES

# ACKNOWLEDGEMENTS

The creation of this book would not be possible without the help of many people who taught, guided, instructed, and corrected me along the way.

Therefore, I would like to begin by expressing my deepest gratitude to the following individuals:

*To Shannon Gonzales-Whitall,* who brought me to church for the very first time.

*To Weston Stutz*, whose sermons ripped the addictions off my soul and filled my heart with grace.

*To the laity of Skyline Wesleyan Church*, whose prayers helped me escape the bondage of Freemasonry.

*To Robert Cornero*, who was the first to mention Orthodoxy to me and encourage me to explore it.

*To Deacon Ezra Ham*, whose lecture series "Finding The Church That Jesus Built" taught me that Orthodoxy is the original Church of Jesus Christ.

*To Father Josiah Trenham*, who convinced me to become a catechumen in the Orthodox Church.

*To Father Simeon Corona*, who baptized me into the Church and taught me how to pray.

*To John Willman*, my friend and spiritual godfather.

*To the laity of St. Gregory of Nyssa Greek Orthodox Church*, who received me into an unknown world and showed me how to navigate it.

*To Karren Olson*, who provided me with many excellent Orthodox resources and helped me work through some of my early questions and objections.

*To Father Gregory-Lazarus Murphy*, whose e-mail to me sparked the revision and rewriting of this book into its present form.

*To my family*, who has loved and supported me no matter how many times I didn't deserve it.

And lastly, I'd like to thank all those who are not named but whom I have met on my journey.

Thank you all for teaching me about history, about sacraments, about patience, about forgiveness, about growth in community and about God and myself.

I am far from the man God wants me to be, but I am closer to becoming him only because of you.

*In the name of the Father, and the Son, and the Holy Spirit.*

*Amen.*

"Woe to those who call evil good and good evil, who put darkness for light and light for darkness, who put bitter for sweet and sweet for bitter."

Isaiah 5:20

# CONTENTS

| | | |
|---|---|---|
| 1 | **Prologue To The Second Edition** | 7 |
| 2 | **Introduction** | 13 |
| 3 | **On Spiritual Warfare** | 20 |
| 4 | **Ideology** | 30 |
| 5 | **Holy And Unholy Mysteries** | 44 |
| 6 | **Light And The Lost Word** | 59 |
| 7 | **Theology** | 65 |
| 8 | **Christology** | 95 |
| 9 | **Soteriology** | 119 |
| 10 | **Masonry And The Churches** | 130 |
| 11 | **Conclusion** | 143 |
| 12 | **About The Author** | 146 |

# PROLOGUE TO THE SECOND EDITION

I first published <u>On The Masons And Their Lies</u> on Pentecost Sunday of 2018. Due to the conversations in my local parish and my efforts online, it slowly began to circulate throughout the Orthodox Christian community. My original intentions in publishing it were to help inform Christians about the spiritual dangers of Freemasonry and to bring curious Freemasons out of the Lodge and into the Church.

Its initial reception was small, but overwhelmingly positive. I realized it was a topic of interest for many people, and the response validated the amount of time and effort I'd put into it to begin with.

However, I received an email from an Orthodox Priest who told me that he'd been struggling with the effects of the Masonic worldview on the hearts and minds of his parishioners. He informed me that, at one point in the history of his parish, nearly every adult male parishioner was also a member of a Masonic Lodge. That un-Christian and anti-Orthodox Masonic mindset, he said, has persisted over the generations - and has formed a barrier to hearing and living the saving Gospel of Jesus Christ.

As a result of the correspondence between he and I on this topic, I decided to reorganize the material as a "handbook" for priests and pastors struggling with this issue. I wanted them to have a ready resource on hand with which to combat the Masonic specter among their laity, giving it out as necessary for careful study and consideration. Therefore, I have completely rearranged the material in this book - and added many parts - in order to best serve that end.

Like the first edition, the second one is written from an Orthodox Christian perspective - but in a way that can be of use to all who call themselves Christians. At various times throughout the book, I will refer to either big-O "Orthodoxy" or small-o "orthodoxy." This distinction is meant to distinguish between those aspects of Christianity which are exclusive to the Orthodox Church, and those beliefs and practices which are common to most mainstream groups.

Many Christian groups have made official statements regarding Freemasonry and whether membership in a Lodge is compatible with their views. I have compiled many such statements into the final chapter of this book, titled **Masonry And The Churches**.

Reorganizing this book meant transforming it from a basic primer into a deeper and fuller exploration of all of Masonry's various anti-Christian sentiments. Many such sentiments are so deeply hidden that even most Masons do not realize they exist. Thus, it is my hope that this book serves to educate not only the Christians reading it, but any Masons who get their hands on it as well.

Before we get into the nuts and bolts of the fraternity and its philosophy, let us cover the first and foremost question: *"What is Freemasonry?"*

If you ask most Masons what Masonry is, they'll give you the scripted response that it's *"a progressive system of morality, veiled in allegory and illustrated by symbols."* Some will tell you that it's *"the world's oldest and largest fraternity,"* while George Washington wrote that *"the grand object of Masonry is to promote the happiness of the human race."*

Regardless of what a man personally believes Masonry to be, the process is always the same: upon joining the fraternity, he will be entering a world of philosophy, of symbolism, of ritual, and of labor. The deeper he goes, the heavier the workload becomes - along with the amount of time which he devotes to it.

A man seeking to join the fraternity is referred to as a "candidate," and receives the first 3 Degrees of Masonry in what is called a "Blue Lodge." Masonic Degrees are mini-plays with actors and speeches, in which the candidate takes part (or which he may simply observe if there is more than one candidate).

After receiving his 3rd Degree in a Blue Lodge, called the *Master Mason* Degree, the man is considered to be a full member of Freemasonry. At that point, he can choose to become an Officer and/or join affiliated groups such as the York Rite, the Scottish Rite, or the Shriners.

If he becomes an Officer, his workload consists not only of memorizing and performing various pieces, but also of increased administrative or supporting duties around his Lodge. The more Masonic groups he joins, the more multiplied these duties become.

In the priest's e-mail, he told me that this seemed to be taking away from the time his parishioners ought to have been devoting to Orthodoxy - and this is a very well-grounded concern. Though many busy people resent this fact, it is simply the reality of life that we have a limited amount of time in which to perform our various tasks and duties.

A man who devotes 10 hours per week to Masonic books has been deprived of 10 hours he may have spent reading those of the Church Fathers. For many Freemasons, the fraternity takes up such a significant portion of their week that they are left with little time to do anything besides work and Masonry.

The fraternity is also designed in such a way that there is no end or limit to the number of duties or roles which any individual Mason may someday take on. There is always a new group, a new Officer role, or a new set of Degrees to consume vast amounts of his attention and time. If a man so desires, he could easily devote his entire life to nothing but Masonry in some form or another.

Generally speaking, other Masons will constantly goad their brethren into taking on as much work as possible. This constant stream of encouragement can be hard to resist, and a man with weak boundaries will quickly find himself devoting many hours to all the various tasks which he has volunteered (or been "volun-told") to do.

In a short amount of time, a zealous Mason may find that Masonry has become the cornerstone of his very existence. It has become his work, his social circle, his relaxation, and his life. And this is precisely where the greatest danger lies; that in having Masonry consume his life, a man may find himself involved in nothing else.

All this time, his mind is being exposed to a particular set of ideas and philosophies which...as you will understand by the time you are done reading this book...cannot possibly deepen his relationship with Jesus Christ as his Lord and Savior. In many ways, Masonry draws men further away from the Christian God rather than closer towards Him.

To believe otherwise is to be ignorant of both Masonry and Christ. To prove to you that this is the case, let us peel back the first veil and see what lies beneath the surface of Freemasonry.

My research for the second edition of <u>On The Masons And Their Lies</u> consisted largely of reading and interpreting Albert Pike's compendium <u>Morals And Dogma</u>, a task which I bitterly hated but believed to be necessary. <u>Morals And</u>

Dogma is a collection of Albert Pike's commentary and thoughts on the first 32 Degrees of the Scottish Rite, which he was largely responsible for designing and revising.

He himself admits that he was *"about equally Author and Compiler"* of the book, as enormous sections of it are simply quoting from other authors on a large variety of topics.

In all fairness, it must be stated that Pike's thoughts are not every Mason's thoughts, as the fraternity itself teaches no strict theological dogma and does not act as a spiritual monolith. However, no American has had such a profound impact on the Scottish Rite as Pike, and I would argue that his understanding of Freemasonry far surpassed that of your average Mason.

I personally believe that many of the ideas which he either writes or cites in Morals And Dogma are the true philosophical underpinning of Freemasonry - and that many in the highest ranks share his beliefs on topics such as Gnosticism, Alchemy, Hermeticism, and Kabbalah.

Many such high-ranking men - Pike included - have openly and publicly admitted that the low-ranking Masons are deliberately misled, while the true philosophical "wisdom" of the fraternity is restricted to its more elite members.

Such statements will be carefully and deliberately unpacked throughout this book.

My other primary sources, in addition to my own personal experience in Freemasonry, are Manly P. Hall's The Secret Teachings Of All Ages and J.D. Buck's Mystical Masonry.

Both of them were 33rd Degree Scottish Rite Masons. It is the highest Degree which the Scottish Rite can bestow, and both of these men had some very troubling things to say about Jesus Christ and those who choose to follow Him.

Due to the vast expanse of Masonic philosophy, I have separated On The Masons And Their Lies into a number of segments. If you are a priest or pastor reading this with the intention of helping men in your parish to leave the Lodge, it will be up to your discernment - and your parishioners' level of understanding - which of these sections to focus on in your efforts.

Thus, this book is meant to illuminate the truth regarding Masonry's **Ideology, Theology, Christology, and Soteriology.** There are additional sections, which I have called **Holy And Unholy Mysteries** and **Light And The Lost Word**, on core differences between Masonry and Christianity which are also crucial to understand.

By the time you are done reading this book, you will know more about Freemasonry than most of its members do. If you are a Roman Catholic or a Protestant reading it, I hope that it also gives you a preview of the grace and beauty available to you within the Orthodox Church, and that it spurs you to inquire further about our ancient faith.

We will begin this journey with a look at Freemasonry's **Ideology**...but before we explore that topic, please allow me to briefly introduce myself.

I did not come across this knowledge by accident, and I hope that my story may serve as a cautionary tale for others.

It is only through my own personal mistakes and errors - combined with God's boundless mercy on me for having made them in my ignorance - that I was eventually able to recognize, identify, and explain the various concepts and ideas which will be detailed to you shortly.

# INTRODUCTION

I was "initiated an Entered Apprentice Mason" on November 17th, 2014. I was "passed to the Degree of Fellowcraft" on December 1st of the same year, and then "raised to the sublime Degree of Master Mason" on January 30th, 2015. I did not realize at the time what a profound effect these events would ultimately have on the course of my life.

I am a man full of sin, utterly unworthy of teaching on the subject of Christianity. And yet God, for reasons known only to Him, allowed me to fall into certain mistakes that I may eventually learn from my errors - and testify against them.

At the time I discovered the Lodge, I was victim to a host of addictions and a wide array of psychological issues. Being totally empty on the inside, I was in a constant state of "seeking" after whatever small morsels of truth I could discover.

That is why I became so captivated by Freemasonry. It presented to me a grand puzzle, only small pieces of which were explained to me at any given time, and my mind latched onto it as onto nothing before. I was led by the hand through a philosophical labyrinth, always believing that the truth I sought was just on the other side of one system or another.

For the first time in my life, I found myself surrounded by men with whom I could talk for hours about many interesting subjects. They were good men, hard workers, and philosophers who taught me an extraordinary amount both directly and simply by socializing with respectable people. They also give an enormous amount of money to charity, in such an organized and successful fashion that the Orthodox Church could - and probably should - take notes as to its efficiency.

I took to the Lodge like a duck to water, and quickly became noticed and respected for my grasp of the various occult and esoteric philosophies which I studied with my brethren. I became an Officer in 4 different bodies, assisted with the conferring of Degrees in the Scottish Rite, and lectured on occult topics to invite-only groups.

These lectures consisted of talks on topics ranging from Hermeticism and the Kabbalah to the symbolism of Baphomet, as I wove together various esoteric streams as best I could. All of this occurred within the span of 2 short years.

In 2016, I published some of my favorite occult material in the book <u>The Secret World Of Freemasonry: The Lost Truth About Freemasons, The Alchemists, And Other Secret Societies</u>. The material consisted largely of lectures I'd delivered in-person, with extra chapters and sections meant to flesh out and connect bits and pieces of a wide range of philosophies.

At its peak, <u>The Secret World Of Freemasonry</u> was the #2 Gnosticism eBook on Amazon - and widely enjoyed by the Masons who read it. Not all of my fraternity brothers appreciated or cared about these topics, but the overall encouragement I received simply guided me deeper and deeper down the rabbit hole.

But then, towards the end of 2016, an incident occurred in my life which I could never have predicted in my wildest dreams. Due to a series of events which is too long and complicated to discuss at the present time, I ended up in a Wesleyan church trying to be healed of my degeneracy and madness.

Suffice it to say that somehow, in the absolute depths of my darkness and despair, God decided in His endless mercy to reach down and show me a better Way. Upon having my heart filled, I suddenly realized just how empty it had previously been. The experience felt roughly like having rolled around in mud all my life, never realizing I was dirty until God came along with a power-hose and washed me anew.

In the words of my patron Saint, Augustine of Hippo, *"My sin was this - that I looked for pleasure, beauty, and truth not in Him but in myself and His other creatures...and the search led me instead to pain, confusion, and error."*

This revelation marked the beginning of my path towards living a more Christian life - and the more I studied Scripture and did my best to pursue holiness, the more powerful my sense of spiritual discernment became. One particular day, which I will never forget, this sense of discernment began to ring my "spiritual alarm bells" in the middle of a Masonic meeting.

As I sat in one of the York Rite's monthly Stated Meetings, looking around me at the other men and Officers clad in red aprons and gesticulating the penalties for the violation of oaths, I was filled with a thick and very heavy sense of dread. As the feeling intensified, my heartbeat sped up and my breathing became both more shallow and more rapid.

I could not explain this feeling at the time, and tried to "shrug it off" as my being in a bad mood or simply having a strange day. I tried my best to dismiss the feeling, and continued attending my usual Masonic meetings. Since I was an Officer in several bodies at the time, I was generally in Lodge a minimum of once or twice per week.

Try as I might to shake the feeling, I just couldn't get rid of it - so after a long and painful process of deliberation, I decided to abandon my position in the Royal Arch (one of the York Rite's sub-groups) in order to resolve the dilemma. While providing me with a brief period of respite from the oppressive energy I had been feeling in that room, my leaving that chair in the Royal Arch ultimately solved nothing.

The same feeling arose again and again every time I stepped foot into the Masonic Lodge, and I eventually came to realize that God simply wanted me to leave the entire organization. My pastor at the time referred to this feeling as "the conviction of the Holy Spirit," and I often felt tugged in two different directions.

This epiphany left me feeling depressed, sad, confused, and unsure of how to proceed. I had spent the past couple of years building a great social circle of people I liked and respected - and who liked and respected me, as well. I was very hesitant to leave it behind…but at the same time, there was no mistaking the calling in my heart.

I spent the next 6 months or so trying to justify a way to stay, sharing my thoughts and feelings with a local Bible Study group and getting their feedback and advice. Once I could no longer rationalize my involvement in Freemasonry, I made the firm decision in my mind and heart to leave the Lodge completely.

And that is when the attacks began.

I am not speaking of physical attacks, or of any kind of intimidation or coercion by the fraternity. Instead, I speak of what I later came to recognize as the *spirit of Masonry itself* doing everything in its power to retain my membership in the organization.

Out of nowhere, crises would pop up that "only I could solve." New groups would invite me in, new honors would await me, and my mind was assaulted by thoughts meant to keep me from straying. The spirit of Masonry worked day and night on me through psychological attacks of this nature, until I eventually gave up the fight and decided to stay.

Fortunately, I was honest enough with myself to realize that my decision was borne of personal weakness - and so I resolved to try again. Deep in prayer, and recognizing my own total inability to win the battle on my own, I begged God to help rescue me from the spiritual quicksand which I had found myself sucked into. I recalled the verse that **"He who is in you is greater than he who is in the world"** (1 John 4:4), and realized that nothing could defeat me with Christ on my side.

Still scared of losing everything I'd worked so hard for, I made one final appeal to God. "*God,*" I cried out, "*if I leave the fraternity I will have no friends. I will have no awards, no honors, no titles, and no social circle. Without Freemasonry, I will have nothing!*"

I received a response, deep in my heart, as if God Himself were saying "*No...you will have ME!*"

With tears pouring out of my eyes, I humbly accepted my destiny. Later that night, I e-mailed the Secretary of my Lodge and informed him of my decision to leave. I am now free of the chains of Freemasonry, and have spent over a year trying to comprehend precisely why God wanted me to leave in the first place.

The book you are about to read is the fruit of those efforts. A large part of its evolution, from my early drafts as a Protestant to its completed form as Orthodox, resulted from my reading the letters of the ancient Church Fathers.

As I explored the writings of the early Church, one thing above all else became abundantly clear to me: the deceptions and heresies which exist in the world today are no different - either in substance or form - than what the Apostles and their students dealt with in the ancient world.

Fascinatingly, I found that many of the arguments I had written against Freemasonry had already been addressed and explored by the Fathers of Christianity. Though the name of Freemasonry had not yet arisen, the concepts underlying it most certainly had.

I began to realize that the same lies have popped up over and over again throughout Church history, each time requiring a new generation of Christian apologetics to help guide the faithful and shield them from going astray.

As we read in **Ecclesiastes 1:9, *"What has been will be again, what has been done will be done again; there is nothing new under the sun."***

Therefore, what you are about to read is nothing new. I am not claiming to invent, innovate, or improve upon what has been said before.

Instead, consider this book to be an old teaching for new eyes. I am simply doing my part to help educate a new generation of Christians on the workings of the Enemy and his minions, that you may remain on guard against them in all their shapes and forms.

More specifically, I am writing to you in order to highlight the particular tactics they use to draw the mind of man away from the Light of Jesus Christ. It is my hope that what you are about to read will help you make sense of what you see around you, and that you may someday give this book to your children and grandchildren as necessity dictates.

I am writing as much for your edification, dear friend in Christ, as I am for the salvation of Masons who are ready to hear the truth.

Make no mistake in believing that they are unreachable; God works as He will, with whom He will, in the ways He will, in the time He will. Many Masons are good men seeking truth, and it is my hope that their understanding of "truth" will ultimately evolve in a more Christian direction.

If you are a Mason reading this book - either because you have been exploring Christianity and seek to learn whether Masonry is compatible with it, or because you intend to write against me and say that I am wrong - then I pray it helps to illuminate your mind and heart, drawing you where God wishes you to go. At some point in this book, if I have done my job well at all, you will realize that you have a choice to make regarding which path to follow.

To the curious Christian, please understand that most Masons are good men. No Masonic Degree preaches behavior which any good man would find offensive - regardless of whether some individual Masons choose to live on their own terms instead - and there is never a call to selfishness, nor to pride, nor to lust.

The Lodge preaches what it calls the "4 cardinal and 3 theological virtues," which are: *temperance, fortitude, prudence, justice, faith, hope, and charity*. Despite the speculation of some, there is not one shred of explicit malice preached within the Masonic fraternity.

But there is far more to Christianity than simply moral and upright behavior, much of which was preached by the pagans as well. Therefore, we must first understand the nature of spiritual warfare before we may proceed any further on our journey.

Let us have a look at how the Enemy works in the minds, hearts, and souls of men.

# ON SPIRITUAL WARFARE

There is a certain sense in which merely being exposed to occult and esoteric concepts can be spiritually dangerous. Even for the most well-grounded Christian - who deliberately reads about them after careful preparation - the Enemy's attacks can be so subtle that a person's mind begins drifting in the wrong direction anyway.

That is why, even before detailing the 4 primary tactics of Satan which I will be highlighting throughout this book, I must give you a word of warning. What you are about to read, particularly in the many quotes you will see from Albert Pike and other Masonic occultists, is some of the most potent spiritual poison ever unleashed upon the world.

It has captivated the minds of some of the world's smartest people, and entire nations have been shaped in its wake. If you go into this material without guarding yourself properly, you may not be able to resist its dark energy from capturing your mind as well.

Even as I read <u>Morals And Dogma</u> in order to research and compile this material for you, I took constant breaks - and asked for constant prayers from those who knew what I was doing - just to maintain good "spiritual hygiene." I am forever grateful for those who assisted me in such a manner.

If at any time during your reading of this book you begin to feel a foreign presence in your mind, heart, or soul, please know that you are *not* imagining things. A developed sense of spiritual discernment is one of the best defenses you can have against Satanic influence, so please trust your gut and take breaks if and when you must.

I further recommend that you pray for protection before each section that you read, perhaps even doing so afterward as well (just to clean out any demonic residue you may have accidentally picked up).

If you are capable of silently praying and reading at the same time, then I recommend mentally repeating the Jesus Prayer as you go: *"Lord Jesus Christ, Son of God, have mercy on me, a sinner."*

The deeper I get into Orthodoxy, the more powerful I realize the Jesus Prayer truly is when it comes to spiritual warfare. With the name of Christ as your sword and humility as your shield, you will be well-prepared for any battle that Satan throws your way.

In this book, I use the term "spiritual warfare" in a very specific sense. I am not referring to the general temptations which plague humanity (the flesh, the world, and the Devil), but instead to a very particular set of tactics which Satan uses to confuse people about the Christian Truth.

To put his actions in context, let us remember the reason that Satan is after us in the first place. To put it simply, he hates us. Why? Because he and his demons are bitterly envious that **"God so loved the world that He gave His only begotten son, that whosoever believes in Him may not perish, but have eternal life." (John 3:16)**

The fallen angels, by way of comparison, are condemned eternally. They cannot escape Hell, they cannot be saved, and they cannot know peace. Therefore, as "misery loves company," they do everything in their power to prevent humanity from achieving that glorious crown which is forever beyond their reach.

As recorded by St. Athanasius in <u>Life Of St. Anthony Of Egypt</u>, St. Anthony once gave a speech to his fellow

Egyptian monks regarding the nature of demons. In that speech, he told them the following:

*"On the one hand they [the demons] deceived the Greeks with their displays, while out of envy of us Christians they move all things in their desire to hinder us from entry into the heavens; in order that we should not ascend up there from whence they fell."*

Thus, when a man or woman decides to follow Christ and attain that holy and spiritual gift which is for us *only*, the demons seethe with rage and hate. Subsequently, they dedicate their full efforts to keeping us in the state in which they, themselves, are eternally trapped.

Strategy flows from goals, and their only goal is stop you from truly knowing God. In order to attain that end, the demons of Masonry make ample use of the following 4 major tactics.

## 1. Perennialism

One of Satan's preferred tactics is to suggest, in one form or another, that what Jesus preached is simply the same thing as what many other people have preached throughout time. This concept is best summarized by the misleading statement "one Light, many paths."

At the core of **Perennialism** is the notion that there is one "true religion," of which all the major world religions are simply imperfect expressions. As you will come to understand as you continue to read this book, **Perennialism** is the very core of occult philosophy. It is often referred to as the "Secret Doctrine" in Masonic and theosophical works, and we will be exploring it in depth later in this book.

In modern times, this occult philosophy is being spread faster and more widely than ever before in history. Technology is a double-edged sword, and one which our Enemy uses to his advantage wherever possible.

It is extremely easy to find videos and "seminars" in which Christ is conflated with many other figures throughout time. Though these are generally debunked very quickly and thoroughly by true Christians, the debunking efforts are not watched nearly as often - and so the damage is done, infecting the minds of both children and adults who simply don't know any better and do not care to pursue the Truth no matter where it leads.

As you will soon see, **Perennialism** is a common belief amongst the highest-ranking Masons. The entire institution is thus infected from the top down, though only those who pay attention come to realize it.

## 2. Salvation Without Christ

The logical endpoint of **Perennialism** is that you don't need Jesus Christ in order to be saved. After all, those who see nothing new in Christ are just as likely to settle on Buddha, Krishna, Dionysus, or St. Germain as their spiritual focus.

The moment they do, Satan has achieved his desired outcome. If he can convince you that Christ is just one of many "Ascended Masters" - a typical term that deceived New Agers use to describe the demons they unknowingly worship and follow - then this will naturally lead you to look elsewhere for salvation.

Our Lord says in **Matthew 7:13-14,** "*Enter through the narrow gate. For wide is the gate and broad is the way that leads to destruction, and many enter through it. But small is the gate and narrow the way that leads to life, and only a few find it.*"

Thus, you may plainly see that the Christian Gospel is exclusive by nature. Subsequently, any appeal to **Salvation Without Christ** is necessarily anti-Christian.

Judging by our Savior's words following these verses, in which He warns against the false prophets whose paths lead to death, it is easy to imagine that He knew the demons would attempt this particular trick.

His ancient warning still rings true today.

Faith in Jesus Christ is a necessary prerequisite to both the process of salvation and the prospect of eternal life in the coming Kingdom of God. Therefore, the Enemy goes to great lengths to convince mankind that we may enjoy eternity by other means.

This trick can take many forms, but the most common in occult circles are *salvation by works* or *salvation anyway*.

*Salvation by works* is the lie that you can be saved simply by being a good person and committing good deeds. *Salvation anyway* is the lie that your soul will enjoy immortality regardless of *either* Christian faith or good deeds, as we see with the heresy of *universalism* (the idea that everyone will be saved, eventually, no matter what).

As you will soon see, Freemasonry often uses both forms of this lie. We know it is a lie because St. Paul writes in **Ephesians 2:8-9, "*For it is by grace you have been saved, through faith - and this is not from yourselves, it is the gift of God - not by works, so that no one can boast.*"**

Only the Enemy and his minions preach salvation by any other means. We will take a closer look at this topic in the chapter on **Soteriology**.

## 3. Distortion And Perversion

Another of the Enemy's favorite tactics is to take holy symbols and convince you that their "true" meaning is something besides what was passed down by the Apostles and their students.

For example, Saints are depicted in icons with a halo around their heads. This represents their attaining *theosis*, the highest and most complete level of union with God.

However, demons may try and convince you that the halo simply represents "the sun." Using elaborate and glittery arguments, they also may try and tell the world that these wonderful Saints and martyrs for Christ were actually just "in touch with their solar chakras."

Or they may take the Cross, and the sacrifice made upon it for all our sakes, and tell you that this story simply symbolizes Christ's "enlightenment."

Though Christ defeated death to save our souls and redeem all creation, demons may tell you that He was simply another mystic who meditated a lot and reached "*nirvana*."

This trick takes as many forms as there are holy symbols, as no route is overlooked in Satan's master plan.

Let us ever remember St. Paul's warning in **Galatians 1:7-8**, "***Evidently some people are throwing you into confusion and trying to pervert the gospel of Christ. But even if we or an angel from heaven should preach a gospel other than the one we preached to you, let them be under God's curse!***"

There is no shortage of false teachers in the world today - even amongst those who call themselves Christian.

## 4. Gnosticism

The **Gnostic** deceptions, prevalent throughout the higher tiers of Masonic philosophy, take two primary forms.

The first is to suggest that Jesus preached "secret teachings" to only a small number of His followers, and that they are the only ones who know the "truth" about Christianity.

Though St. Irenaeus already wrote volumes refuting this lie, it remains popular even today. Wherever you hear it preached, know that it was born of occult influence.

The second form of the **Gnosticism** deception is to try and convince the unwary that God does not exist *outside* of you, but is rather a symbol for "who you are" at the deepest level of your being. They will tell you that "God is the underlying source of everything, and who you are in your core."

Rather than the Biblical God - who created the world as separate from Himself (though His energies permeate and sustain creation) - this second **Gnostic** deception preaches that God *is* the world itself.

This pantheistic view of God and His relationship with humanity is not what Christianity preaches, and it causes many problems.

For example, if God only exists within you…if, in fact, there is nothing which you yourself are not…then what need would you have for salvation? What need would there be for prayer?

What would there be to be saved from, and why would Christ have come at all?

This "God and Christ are just symbols for inner states of being" idea is a very transparent lie to those strong in faith and Christian understanding, but very seductive and misleading to those who are not.

The Enemy goes to extraordinary and complex lengths to make these 4 tactics seem like sound scholarship, logical conclusions, and any other form of "sensible" which he can possibly make them out to be.

That is why I have written <u>On The Masons And Their Lies</u>: to place a stumbling block before Satan, and expose his lies with the power of the Spirit and the truth.

By these efforts, it is my hope that the Holy Spirit illuminates the nature of the Masonic deception and - if you yourself are a Mason reading this - causes you to rethink your affiliation.

Should this book stir up your conscience and you become convicted of your activities in the Masonic Lodge, know that leaving will not be easy.

The spirit of Masonry will do everything in its power to keep you in its grasp…as it did to me…through whatever means it believes will be most likely to stop you from leaving.

For as St. Anthony describes the demons, "*…they are treacherous, and are ready to change themselves into all forms and assume all appearances.*"

They will tell you that you are turning your back on your friends who love you, that you are breaking your commitments to a fraternity which has done many good things for you…and it may even promote you to new stations and invite you into new groups.

Whichever of your heartstrings are the most sensitive, such are those the Devil will pluck.

There is a war being waged for your soul, and only one side can win. The Christian path is full of hard choices, in which we are asked to sacrifice *something* for He who sacrificed *all* for us.

And while this path is difficult every step of the way, those who trust in God's promises and benevolence will find themselves rewarded with the fruits of the Holy Spirit, with inner peace of mind and heart, and with the ability to defeat temptation before it even has a chance to set in.

The greater the sacrifice you make for Him, the greater degree of wisdom and understanding you will receive. Therefore, if you decide to leave the Lodge after reading this book, take it from me that what awaits you on the other side is so far superior to what you leave behind that it defies description. It may be scary to think about what you're being asked to do...but if you can bring yourself to do it, I promise that you will never look back.

Remember and be strengthened by the fact that "**He who is in you is stronger than he who is in the world.**" **(1 John 4:4)** God fights on our behalf, so we do not have to face the Enemy alone.

With an understanding of the 4 major tactics which Satan uses in Freemasonry to confuse and deceive, let us begin to examine the fraternity in depth. Keep in mind that everything I have written about is publicly-available knowledge, to be found in published books and the statements of prominent Masons.

Using that information, let us begin our journey with an exploration of Freemasonry's **Ideology**.

"Enter through the narrow gate. For wide is the gate and broad is the road that leads to destruction, and many enter through it. But small is the gate and narrow the road that leads to life, and only a few find it."

Matthew 7:13-14

# IDEOLOGY

This chapter will explore Freemasonry's **Ideology** from a number of different angles, seeking to establish the truth regarding its views on religion, politics, and even the nature of truth itself. We will begin with the nature of truth.

Differences of opinion on religion, politics, spirituality - and even life itself - generally boil down to a difference of opinion on the nature of truth itself. Does objective truth exist, or do we create it as we go? Is one man's truth any more valid than another's? Indeed, the entire spectrum of beliefs is stretched between the poles of subjective vs. objective truth.

On one side, there are those who believe that reality does not exist apart from our perception of it - and that the world should subsequently conform to the desires and passions of each individual as he or she sees fit. This cannot work, of course, since every individual is different in fundamental and important ways...but this nuance tends to escape those who believe the world should conform itself to what we personally desire it to be.

On the other side, there are those who believe that objective reality exists - as instituted and designed by God Himself - and that the key to life is subsequently to conform ourselves to that truth to the greatest possible extent. Rather than doubling down on our own desires and preferences, those of us on this more traditional side believe in personally sacrificing all of our own beliefs and tendencies which we find to be out of alignment with God's eternal Truth.

Without getting too deep into philosophical speculation, I mention this only to highlight one of the primary ways in which Satan attacks those who might otherwise become good and faithful Christians.

Christ says that He is the Truth; Satan responds by asking whether such a thing really exists in the first place.

This subtle chipping-away at the idea of truth, be it religious or spiritual or political, is one of the key methods by which Freemasonry weakens and softens the minds of its members. Before its own ideas can take root in a man's mind, it must first get him to question what he believes in the first place.

Therefore, it should not surprise us to hear Albert Pike, commenting on the *Fellowcraft* Degree, stating that *"No man or body of men can be infallible, and authorized to decide what other men shall believe, as to any tenet of faith. Except to those who first receive it, every religion and the truth of all inspired writings depend on human testimony and internal evidences, to be judged of by Reason and the wise analogies of Faith. Each man must necessarily have the right to judge of their truth for himself; because no man can have any higher or better right to judge than another of equal information and intelligence."*

In his commentary on the 10th Degree, *Illustrious Elect Of The Fifteen*, Pike further writes that *"No human being can with certainty say, in the clash and conflict of hostile faiths and creeds, what is truth, or that he is surely in possession of it, so everyone should feel that it is quite possible that another[,] equally honest and sincere with himself, and yet holding the contrary opinion, may himself be in possession of the truth, and that whatever one firmly and conscientiously beliefs, is truth, to him."*

This personal method of arriving at religious truth amounts to little more than "what you sincerely believe." If you feel like it's true, it's true - and therefore, there is no objective truth. Divine revelation and the pronouncements of the Holy Spirit through the Prophets, in Pike's paradigm, have no higher authority on truth than what any given person may sincerely think or feel at any given time. Presumably, if a person believes a thing to be true at one time in his life - and then another thing to be true at a later stage - then both things are equally true, *for him*, utterly without regard to whether they are true *at all*.

He further chips away at the idea of revealed and objective truth in his commentary on the 28th Degree, *Knight Of The Sun or Prince Adept*. In a section called "Freemasonry Not Dogmatic," Pike writes that *"We have hitherto, in the instruction of the several Degrees, confined ourselves to laying before you the great thoughts that have found expression in the different ages of the world, leaving you to decide for yourself as to the orthodoxy or heterodoxy of each, and what proportion of truth, if any, each contained."*

Pike puts human reasoning on par with Divinely-revealed Truth, elevating man's role to that of God Himself. It insults the Martyrs who shed their blood to share the Gospel, and distracts a man from the only path to true *theosis*. After all, none of the Saints simply reasoned their way to Heaven.

Just as importantly, what Freemasonry preaches to its lower-level members (and those outside the fraternity completely) is not necessarily what it preaches to those whom it considers the philosophical "elite" within its halls. Before we can proceed any further, understand this: what Masonry tells the world is not what Masonry tells its higher-ups.

In his commentary on the 3rd Degree, *Master Mason*, Pike openly claims that *"Masonry, like all the Religions, all the Mysteries, Hermeticism and Alchemy, conceals its secrets from all except the Adepts and Sages, or the Elect, and uses false explanations and misinterpretations of its symbols to mislead those who deserve only to be misled...So Masonry jealously conceals its secrets, and intentionally leads conceited interpreters astray."*

Henry Clausen, a later 33rd Degree Sovereign Grand Commander of the Scottish Rite, agrees with Pike that *"an Initiate may imagine he understands the ethics, symbols and enigmas, whereas a true explanation of these is reserved for the more adept."*

As this book continues, we will explore in depth what sorts of ideas are *"reserved for the more adept."* The deeper we go into its secret teachings, the more obvious it will become that these teachings are not compatible with the Christian Gospel. But let us not get ahead of ourselves.

I also cannot overemphasize that, when I mention the names of such men as Pike and Clausen and Lévi and Hall and Buck in this book, I am not under the mistaken impression that they spoke for themselves; you must understand that when I write of "their" statements and opinions, what I truly refer to is the demons which were speaking and writing through them. I find it unlikely that any of these men had the necessary spark of life within them by which we might attribute their thoughts to any other cause, and it should be understood that they were so spiritually devastated - so absolutely, thoroughly, and completely hollowed-out by their occult practices - that by the time they published their works, their bodies were nothing but vessels for the dark spirits which possessed them.

For the Apostle writes that **"our struggle is not against flesh and blood, but against the rulers, against the authorities, against the powers of this dark world and against the spiritual forces of evil in the heavenly realms."** *(***Ephesians 6:12)**

It should always be understood, therefore, that these men do not speak on their own behalf - but are rather puppets of forces which are beyond their power to contain or comprehend.

And as it is the very nature of demons to deceive, we should not be surprised to find many high-ranking Masons openly admitting that the fraternity lies to those of its members who it perceives to be stupid - but useful - cannon fodder. To the philosophical elite of Masonry, these "mundane" Masons simply exist to pay dues and keep the Lodges running.

If you are a pastor or priest who has purchased this book in order to help a man out of the Lodge, you must first discern whether he is of the higher or lower order of Masons. If he is of the higher order, you will be combatting with a higher degree of possession - and if he is of the lower order, he likely does not even understand what he's involved with in the first place. You must therefore carefully try and figure out which group he belongs to, praying for him and directing his mind and soul as necessary.

Be warned, however, that he is likely to display a strong defensive stance when you begin to confront him about the truth of Freemasonry. He has been trained to think and respond in certain ways to attacks against the Lodge and its ideals, and you will likely encounter this very early on in your attempts to help him. Remember you are fighting a demon - not the man himself - and that prayer is often more powerful than persuasion.

The next logical question to ask is this: *If Masonry teaches one philosophy to its "adepts" and another to those it considers too stupid to understand it, what is that Masonry says to the world?*

## How Masonry Presents Itself

In the Introduction to <u>Morals And Dogma</u>, Pike states that *"Masonry is the great Peace Society of the world. Wherever it exists, it struggles to prevent international difficulties and disputes; and to bind Republics, Kingdoms, and Empires together in one great band of peace and amity."*

He later elaborates that *"To us the whole world is God's Temple, as is every upright heart. To establish all over the world the New Law and Reign of Love, Peace, Charity, and Toleration, is to build that Temple, most acceptable to God, in erecting which Masonry is now engaged."*

Thus, you may see that Masonry as an institution - far more than a simple fraternal organization - has specific political and spiritual goals which it is actively working to achieve throughout the world.

As noble their stated goals may sound on paper, however, they quickly run into the very real differences between groups which often keep them at arms' length from one another. In order to solve this problem, Masonry is designed to eliminate from its rituals and teachings anything which may elevate one system of beliefs above any other.

Of course, it also usurps the role of God in deciding what is "most acceptable" to Him in the first place. As will be continually unfolded to you as you read this book, Masonry's particular view of that topic is often at odds with what the Christian faith teaches.

In order to join a Lodge, a man must simply meet the following requirements: he must be "of good character," he must believe in "a Supreme Being and an afterlife," and he must be at least "18 years of age." Beyond these requirements, a man is free to be and believe whoever and whatever he wishes.

Further, Masons are strictly prohibited from speaking to each other about religion or politics while inside the boundaries of a Masonic Lodge. These topics are considered "divisive," and the prohibition of their discussion is meant to maintain harmony between members of various political and spiritual leanings.

This "solution" inherently and deliberately denies that any particular creed is the sole possessor of Truth, which as you have seen, is taught to Masons throughout the various Degrees of the fraternity. Further, it simply sweeps important topics under the rug rather than address them directly.

Such a creed, while appearing to simply respect all mens' personal "right" to decide what is true or not for himself, obviously denies the role of the Holy Spirit in protecting, maintaining, and dogmatizing the truths of the Christian faith.

A Council may declare that Christ is God, while another man's reason and logic may lead him to believe that He is not. In Pike's eyes, there is no essential difference between these two conclusions - and no reason to believe that either view is more correct than the other.

In fact, Pike quotes rarely from the Church Fathers - but regularly from Gnostics and heretics like Arius, Simon Magus, Bardesanes, Valentinus, and Basilides.

These sentiments are nothing but a subtle assault on the idea that objective religious Truth exists. It is to place oneself on the same pedestal as the Holy Fathers of the Church, deciding on one's own whether their dogmas were correct or not. In a certain sense, Freemasonry is Protestantism on steroids.

As if to prove the point, Pike later writes that Masonry *"reverences all the great reformers. It sees in Moses, the Lawgiver of the Jews, in Confucius and Zoroaster, in Jesus of Nazareth, and in the Arabian Iconoclast, Great Teachers of Morality, and Eminent Reformers, if no more: and allows every brother of the Order to assign to each such higher and even Divine Character as his Creed and Truth require."*

Manly P. Hall echoes Pike's religious indifference, stating that *"The true Mason is not creed-bound. He realizes with the divine illumination of his lodge that as a Mason his religion must be universal: Christ, Buddha or Mohammed, the name means little, for he recognizes only the light and not the bearer. He worships at every shrine, bows before every altar, whether in temple, mosque or cathedral, realizing with his truer understanding the oneness of all spiritual truth...No true Mason can be narrow, for his Lodge is the divine expression of all broadness."*

Such **Perennialist** poison should immediately set off the alarms of all sane and sober Christians. How could the name of Christ "mean little," when Scripture tells us it is the **"name above all other names?" (Philippians 2:9)**

More importantly, why would Masonry so casually dismiss the name of the Son of God, the only name that makes demons flee in terror, unless it was specifically trying to get you not to wield its power?

A man who believes there is no difference between Christ, Buddha, and Mohammad has already suffered devastating defeat at the hands of demons - and does not even realize how far he is from victory in the unseen warfare.

In his excellent book <u>Orthodoxy And Heterodoxy</u>, Father Andrew Stephen Damick correctly observes that *"To assert that all religions are really just different paths to God is to do violence to the fundamental beliefs of these religions. The Hindu yogi trying to achieve dissolution of self and absorption into the universe is not on the same path as the Jew bowing down before the God of Abraham, Isaac, and Jacob, or the Scientologist working to become 'clear' of alien beings called 'thetas.' To suggest that all these believers are really on the same path is to do damage to their theological systems - to assert that we know better than these people do what their teachings really are."*

Therefore, **Perennialism** should be seen not as a friendly ecumenical circle where members of different religions can gather round the campfire and sing "kumbaya" hand-in-hand, but rather for what it truly is: a direct attack on the foundation of our faith.

Our Lord said to us that *"I am the way, and the truth, and the life. No man comes to the Father except through me."* **(John 14:6)** If you believe that He was telling the truth, then you cannot also believe that Jews, Muslims, Hindus, and Buddhists are going to enjoy eternal life with God on account of their high morality or good deeds in general. People living in the age of sensibility and feelings do not often want to acknowledge this, but *you have to choose*.

It should also give Christians a moment of pause to consider that we are called to the Great Commission, to *"go and make disciples of all nations, baptizing them in the name of the Father and of the Son and of the Holy Spirit."* **(Matthew 28:19)** How can a man spread the Gospel of Jesus Christ to the world while simultaneously believing that he has no right to tell another what to believe?

The answer, of course, is that he cannot. This creates a conflict whereby each Christian Mason must decide whether Christianity is true and worth spreading, or whether he is bound by Masonic oath not to do so.

This kind of relativism - that whatever we subjectively believe to be true is equal in value to what anyone else subjectively believes to be true - has come to dominate our entire cultural paradigm when it comes to the topic of faith. It is not difficult to trace the spread of this kind of thinking back to the times and places in which Masonry takes root, and one could accurately state that the liberal Enlightenment was simply the political application of Masonic philosophy.

## Is Masonry A Religion?

Despite its proclamations to respect everyone's "individual truth," it cannot be denied that Masonry claims to possess particular "truths" of its own. In his commentary on the 8th Degree, *Intendant Of The Building*, Pike goes so far as to say that "*It is the province of Masonry to teach all truths - not moral truth alone, but political and philosophical, and even religious truths, so far as concerns the great and essential principles of each.*"

As <u>Morals And Dogma</u> goes on, it becomes clearer and clearer that the fraternity...while claiming to respect equally all creeds and faiths...does in fact believe that there is one "true religion" of which the others are branches at best (and ignorant perversions at worst). For example, Pike later asserts that Masonry is "*the universal, eternal, immutable religion, such as God planted it in the heart of universal humanity...The ministers of this religions are all Masons who comprehend it and are devoted to it; its sacrifices to God are good works, the sacrifices of the base and disorderly passions, the offering up of self-interest on the altar of humanity, and perpetual efforts to attain to all the moral perfection of which man is capable.*"

The tenets of this "true religion" will be explored more carefully in the chapter on **Theology**. For now, let us simply consider what Pike writes in his commentary on the 18th Degree, *Knight Rose Croix*.

In that section, he writes that "*The Degree of Rose Croix teaches three things - the unity, immutability, and goodness of God; the immortality of the Soul; and the ultimate defeat and extinction of evil and wrong and sorrow, by a Redeemer or Messiah, yet to come, if he has not already appeared.*"

To any genuine Christian believer, the above comment should appear rather bizarre. It is the foundational tenet of our faith that Christ *is* the Messiah, that He *has* come, and that He *will* come again *as Christ*. There is no "if," there is no "maybe," and there is no "other" Redeemer. By implying that the Messiah may not yet have come, Pike's demon is simply lowering the work of Christ in order to get you looking elsewhere for salvation.

A Christian man, receiving the 18th Degree, is being asked to consider whether the messianic figure looked forward to by Jews or Muslims might just be the one to save the world after all. He is being asked to give up a central pillar of his faith in order to not "offend" men of other belief systems.

He, therefore, must make a choice which is presented to men in the Lodge over and over again throughout their participation in it: *do you believe in the Gospel of Jesus Christ?* And as a followup... *do you believe in it so powerfully that you're willing to face the judgment of others for His sake?*

In just a moment, we will examine the Masonic religion in more depth. But before we get there, I'd like to make one last point about the **Ideology** espoused by Albert Pike and the Masonic institution.

## Liberty, Equality, Fraternity

The phrase "Liberty, Equality, Fraternity" comes up many times throughout both <u>Morals And Dogma</u> and Pike's other writings. It is mentioned in the Degrees of the Scottish Rite, and encapsulates the political, spiritual, and religious views of Albert Pike and the demon which operates through him.

He described the fraternity by saying that "*In every age, its device has been 'Liberty, Equality, Fraternity,' with constitutional government, law, order, discipline, and subordination to legitimate authority - government and not anarchy.*"

He elaborated on this idea in his essay <u>What Masonry Is</u>, claiming that Masonry is the preacher *"of Liberty, that is not License, nor Anarchy, nor Licentiousness, nor the Despotism of party; and by which men are free, but not too free: of Fraternity, in that sober sense which regards men as the children of a common Father, to be loved when good, pitied and not hated when bad, persuaded and not persecuted when in error: of Equality, in the eye of the Law, in political rights and in the rights of conscience."*

Pike marched under the banner of "Liberty, Equality, Fraternity" - and bade his Masonic minions to do likewise. Few would argue that, as described, it superficially appears to promote wholesome and righteous values. After all, who would not want to live in a society based on brotherhood and fairness?

Yet the Frenchman Louis de Bonald said that *"The cry 'Liberty, Equality, Fraternity or Death!' was much in vogue during the Revolution. Liberty ended by covering France with prisons, equality by multiplying titles and decorations, and fraternity by dividing us. Death alone prevailed."*

The same sentiment was expressed more recently by Roy Campbell when he said that *"More people have been imprisoned for Liberty, humiliated and tortured for Equality, and slaughtered for Fraternity in this century, than for any less hypocritical motives during the Middle Ages."*

If it is true that **"every tree is known by its fruit" (Luke 6:44)**, then it should be plain as day that Masonry's relativistic philosophy is a very rotten tree indeed.

Thus we see can see that the result of Pike's philosophy is not "liberty, equality, fraternity" but rather "division, elitism, persecution." What Pike writes most fervently against becomes precisely that to which Masonic **Ideology** leads in practice.

You have now learned that Freemasonry whittles away at the notion of objective Truth in order to implant its lies more firmly in the mind.

You have learned that it preaches religious indifference to the world outside, while reserving its own secret religion for its high-ranking "adepts." Soon, you will know more about this secret religion than the overwhelming majority of Freemasons do.

Finally, you have learned that its political philosophy has resulted in widespread pain and suffering. We must judge not by words and intentions, but rather by actions and results.

With all this out of the way, we may now go a level deeper into the truth about what Masonry is and how it operates. While it has made many claims as to its origins throughout time, many such claims have been debunked via modern scholarship on the topic.

Therefore, there is no specific institution which we can point to and say "That is where Freemasonry began." We may, however, point to its philosophical and spiritual ancestors across various times and ages - where the same teachings were reiterated, in one form or another, to the initiates of various pagan Mystery Schools throughout the ancient world.

So without further ado, let us take a closer look at the **Holy And Unholy Mysteries**.

"The devil baptizes some, that is, his believers and faithful ones, promising remission of sins after immersion; and if my memory serves, Mithra there sets a mark on the forehead of his soldiers, celebrates the oblation of bread, introduces a symbol of the resurrection, and under the sword wreathes a crown."

Tertullian, Prescription Against Heretics

# HOLY AND UNHOLY MYSTERIES

It has now been demonstrated to you that, despite the claims of many Masons that Freemasonry is not a religion, such a sentiment is not shared by those men in the higher ranks. Many 33rd Degree Scottish Rite Masons have emphatically declared that Masonry *is* a religion (an opinion shared by many Christians who have studied the topic in-depth), and it teaches what it believes to be pure, primitive truths "untainted" by the Saints and Holy Fathers of the Christian faith.

You have also seen that the political philosophy which follows from those spiritual "truths" tends to end in disaster whenever and wherever it is implemented - a prime example of the "fruit of the rotten tree" idea in action. In this chapter, we will examine the forms and history of the Masonic religion: where it claims to come from, whose ideas it claims to reiterate, and most insidiously of all - the many ways in which it attempts to equate itself with Orthodox Christianity.

You will discover this to be a common theme throughout Masonic philosophy; the deliberate, dishonest conflation of its own teachings with those of the Church is just another means by which Satan attempts to mislead men and set them on the wrong path. After all, if Masonry is more or less the same as Orthodoxy anyway, then there is really no reason to leave the Lodge…right?

To demonstrate what I mean, consider the following passage as written in <u>Morals And Dogma</u> by the present edition's editor, Arturo De Hoyos. He writes in the Introduction that *"The early Church Fathers stated that certain beliefs and practices came from the Apostles, who prescribed that they be preserved only by oral tradition. St. Basil referred to symbolic gestures, washings, and anointings as among the 'unpublished and secret teachings which the fathers guarded in a silence out of the reach of curious meddlings and inquisitive investigation'...[this] demonstrates that hidden or secret teachings, or unfamiliar ritual practices, are not necessarily contrary to the purposes of the Christian faith, and that beliefs or practices which are unfamiliar should not be condemned outright.*"

While it is certainly true that oral traditions exist in the hierarchy of the Orthodox Church, it is equally true that these traditions have nothing to do with the astrological or alchemical "secrets" of which some Masons claim they consist. St. Basil clarified what he meant by asking "*Which of the saints has left us in writing the words of the invocation at the displaying of the bread of the Eucharist and the cup of blessing? For we are not, as is well known, content with what the apostle or the Gospel has recorded, but both in preface and conclusion we add other words as being of great importance to the validity of the ministry, and these we derive from unwritten teaching…On what written authority do we do this? Is not our authority silent and mystical tradition? Nay, by what written word is the anointing of oil itself taught? And whence comes the custom of baptizing thrice? And as to the other customs of baptism from what Scripture do we derive the renunciation of Satan and his angels? Does not this come from that unpublished and secret teaching which our fathers guarded in a silence out of the reach of curious meddling and inquisitive investigation?*"

Therefore, you may clearly see that the "secret teachings" of Orthodoxy generally refer to specific gestures, words of invocation, and methods of baptism. There is also, of course, an unspeakable Mystery of which Orthodox Christians take part as we learn and grow in Christ through a life of asceticism and sacramental grace.

However, the "secret teachings" of the ancient Mystery schools were concerned with entirely different topics than those of the Orthodox Church - a detail that Pike and De Hoyos would prefer that you not notice.

Instead, they wish you to believe that that there is no essential difference between what the ancient Christian Church taught and what came before it; that it is simply the same old teaching wrapped in new clothes, with its *real* meaning reserved only for the intellectual elite.

In fact, Pike regularly uses the unwritten traditions of the Orthodox Church as a springboard from which to deliver his absurdity. A prime example of this comes from his commentary on the 17th Degree, Knight Of The East And West, in which he quotes heavily from Azariah Pierson's Traditions Of Freemasonry and Jacques Matter's Critical History Of Gnosticism.

Blending passages from these two books together, Pike writes that *"the writings of the Apostles were incomplete...they contained only the germs of another doctrine, which must receive from the hands of philosophy, not only the systematic arrangement which was wanting, but all the development which lay concealed therein. The writings of the Apostles, [early Christians] said, in addressing themselves to mankind in general, enunciated only the articles of the vulgar faith; but transmitted the mysteries of knowledge to superior minds, to the Elect - mysteries handed down from generation to generation in esoteric traditions; and to this science of the mysteries they have given the name of 'Gnosis.'"*

In the following chapters, you will learn precisely what Pike means when he refers to esoteric **Gnostic** traditions. As you read, keep in mind that the Scottish Rite's official position on the religion of Albert Pike is that he was a Christian all his life.

In his commentary on the 28th Degree, *Knight Of The Sun or Prince Adept*, Pike writes that *"In the Mysteries, wherever they were practiced, was taught that truth of the primitive revelation, the existence of One Great Being, Infinite and pervading the Universe, Who was there worshipped without superstition; and His marvelous nature, essence, and attributes taught to the Initiates; while the vulgar attributed His works to Secondary Gods, personified, and isolated from Him in fabulous independence."*

These were, in fact, taught by many of the ancient pagan Mystery Schools. In language which Pike very clearly borrowed from, Pierson notes that Initiates *"were taught the truths of primitive revelation, the existence and attributes of one God, the immortality of the Soul, rewards and punishments in a future life, the phenomena of Nature, the arts, the sciences, morality, legislation, philosophy, and philanthropy, and what we now style psychology and metaphysics, with animal magnetism, and the other occult sciences."*

As you can see, the philosophical position of the Masonic "adepts" is essentially that the one "true religion" has been taught in Mystery Schools all throughout the ages, and that the Christian Church is just "the same old thing" using new language and imagery. If you were to listen to possessed Masonic occultists on this topic, they would try and convince you that the Apostles were simply Initiates in yet another pagan Mystery cult, who lied to the masses of Christian disciples about the true nature of the Gospel.

Such conflation of the Divine Mysteries with unholy pagan rituals is a regular feature of Masonic philosophy, as the demons seek to plant seeds of **Gnosticism** in whatever soil may be ripe. Of course, it must be said that such ideas can only take hold in minds which, through indulgence in sin and laziness toward the true Christian life, are susceptible to demonism in the first place.

Just as mosquitos can thrive and settle only in swamps, Masonry can only thrive in the swamp of our negligence.

In order to continue his assault on Christianity by way of **Distortion And Perversion**, Pike also quotes from History Of Free-Masonry In Europe by Emmanuel Rebold. As usual, his intention is to convince the naive reader that Christianity is nothing but recycled paganism.

He begins by commenting on the form of the ancient Christian religion, writing that *"In the early days of Christianity, there was an initiation like those of the pagans. Persons were admitted on special conditions only. To arrive at a complete knowledge of the doctrine, they had to pass three degrees of instruction. The initiates were consequently divided into three classes; the first, Auditors, the second, Catechumens, and the third, the Faithful. The Auditors were a sort of novices, who were prepared by certain ceremonies and certain instruction to receive the dogmas of Christianity. A portion of these dogmas was made known to the Catechumens; who, after particular purifications, received baptism, or the initiation of the theogenesis (divine generation); but in the grand mysteries of that religion, the incarnation, nativity, passion, and resurrection of Christ, none were initiated but the Faithful. These doctrines, and the celebration of the Holy Sacraments, particularly the Eucharist, were kept with profound secrecy."*

It is accurate to say that the Orthodox Christian Church conceals its Mysteries from the uninitiated. St. Cyril of Jerusalem wrote in his Catechesis that *"The splendor of glory is for those who are early enlightened: obscurity and darkness are the portion of the unbelievers and ignorant. Just so the church discovers its Mysteries to those who have advanced beyond the class of Catechumens: we employ obscure terms with others."*

Orthodoxy has never denied that it reserves certain doctrines and Sacraments for only those initiated into the Church via baptism, as commanded by Christ Himself when He said *"Do not give what is holy to dogs, or throw your pearls before swine."* **(Matthew 7:6)**

But it is false that the story of the passion and resurrection of Christ were not taught to the masses. St. Paul wrote to the Corinthian Church that *"When I came to you, brothers, I did not come with eloquence or wisdom as I proclaimed to you the testimony about God. For I decided to know nothing when I was with you except Jesus Christ and Him crucified."* **(1 Corinthians 2:1-2)**

This was the primary message preached by the Apostles: that Jesus Christ, God in the flesh, had died for our sins and been resurrected to save us from death. This is the Gospel which we are called to preach to every nation and tribe on the planet.

Furthermore, what Pike and his brethren fail to understand - assuming they are not deliberately lying in the first place - is that Christianity has long explained the similarities between its forms and those of the pagan religions which came before it. These similarities are not a novel concept, nor are they proof of any sort of equality between the two sets of beliefs.

Indeed, there can be no denying that these parallels exist. The early Church recognized it, wrote about it, and made clear statements which both respected what the ancient Mystery Schools got correct and rejected what they did not.

St. Justin Martyr, in the first half of the second century, was just such a man. Having converted from paganism to Orthodox Christianity as an educated adult, he always maintained his respect for philosophy - while recognizing that it was only truly fulfilled in Christ.

He described pagan philosophy as "*a schoolmaster to bring us to Christ*," noting that all Truth - wherever it may be found - is indeed from God.

This brings up the obvious question: *If the forms and sacraments of the Orthodox Church were prefigured by those of the ancient pagan philosophical schools, how can we explain such a phenomenon?*

To that end, I offer two possibilities. The true answer may be one, the other, or some combination of the two.

Firstly, I find it reasonable to suggest that, just as the Old Covenant prepared the Jews for the coming Incarnation of Jesus Christ, the Gentiles were also being prepared for His coming through certain aspects of their own religions. For just as the early Jewish converts saw in Christ their awaited Messiah and the pure Lamb of God, perhaps the ancient Gentile converts saw in Him their own awaited Redeemer who came to conquer death.

This could explain why the 3 Magi were looking for Christ in the first place; after all, the Zoroastrians were seeking a Messiah they called the *Sosiosch*. Having been taught where and when to seek Him by the tenets of their own pagan faith, they were eventually led to Christ.

It is clear from the historical record that many of the pagan Mystery Schools taught monotheism, the immortality of the soul, divine reward for virtue, and the improvement of the human character. I find it safe to say that Christ has fulfilled all of these previous systems, making them as obsolete for the Gentiles as the Old Covenant has become for the Jews.

Therefore, to involve oneself in such matters today is to seek that which has already come; it is to move backwards through time, ever searching for He who arrived more than 2,000 years ago.

The other possibility regarding the similarities of the Christian and pagan systems is that, knowing ahead of time what form the Church would ultimately take, the demons took it upon themselves to mimic what was foretold by the Prophets. This seems to be the view promoted by St. Justin.

By doing so, they could simply point to the religions they had founded and say "We already have that! No need for another school teaching monotheism and immortality." Perhaps, by this method, they sought to maintain members amongst their ranks who may otherwise have converted to Christianity.

As mentioned, I do not know whether the truth is one, both, or some combination of these possibilities. All I know is that the forms and teachings of the pagan Mystery Schools have nothing to offer a man who seeks Christ in His fullness.

To demonstrate to you the lengths that demons have gone to in their efforts to persuade men away from the Truth, let us continue our examination of the religion of Masonry. Pike once said that *"Masonry is identical to the ancient Mysteries,"* so let us look at precisely what he meant.

If you will recall from our previous discussion of Satan's 4 favorite tactics to use within the halls of Freemasonry, **Salvation Without Christ** plays a major role in his strategy. As such, it is only reasonable that the demonic religions which he instituted would outwardly preach good behavior and moral virtue.

Not only do such men tend to have better reputations from which to espouse Satanic philosophy to the world, but the seductive nature of believing that we are saved by good deeds is a powerful trap indeed.

Therefore, I'd like to draw your attention to Pike's commentary on the 26th Degree, *Prince Of Mercy Or Scottish Trinitarian*. In that section, Pike includes a Masonic catechism in the form of a question-and-answer session between two Officers of the Lodge. That catechism contains the following exchange:

**Question:** *What are the symbols of the purification necessary to make us perfect Masons?*

**Answer***: Lavation with pure water, or baptism; because to cleanse the body is emblematical of purifying the soul; and because it conduces to the bodily health, and virtue is the health of the soul, as sin and vice are its malady and sickness: unction, or anointing with oil, because thereby we are set apart and dedicated to the service and priesthood of the Beautiful, the True, and the Good: and robes of white, emblems of candor, purity and truth.*

**Question:** *What is the chief symbol of man's ultimate redemption and regeneration?*

**Answer:** *The fraternal supper, of bread which nourishes, and of wine which refreshes and exhilarates, symbolical of the time to come, when all mankind shall be one great harmonious brotherhood; and teaching us these great lessons: that as matter changes ever, but no single atom is annihilated, it is not rational to suppose that the far nobler soul does not continue to exist beyond the grave...And thus, in the bread we eat, and in the wine we drink tonight may enter into and form part of us the identical particles of matter that once formed parts of the material bodies called Moses, Confucius, Plato, Socrates, or Jesus of Nazareth.*

This type of Satanic "eucharist" also takes place during the 14th Degree, *Grand Elect, Perfect, And Sublime Mason*. Rather than being deified through the Body and Blood of Jesus Christ, the Masonic candidate is simply "becoming one with the more noble souls of the past."

It mocks the Real Presence of Christ in the true Eucharist, in which Orthodox Christianity has believed since the Last Supper, lowering such an act to being merely "symbolical" of a future age. Given that the Orthodox life largely revolves around the Holy Gifts, and the reception of the Body and Blood of Jesus Christ in the Eucharist, it is easy to see that Freemasonry is little more than a perverted shadow of the institution which it seeks to imitate.

Worse yet, the ancient Mystery teachings are often precisely the magical arts which God condemns from Genesis to Revelation. In his commentary on the 23rd Degree, *Chief Of The Tabernacle*, Pike quotes from Jean-Marie Ragon's Masonic Orthodoxy that "*Among the sciences taught by Hermes, there were secrets which he communicated to the Initiates only upon condition that they should bind themselves, by a terrible oath, never to divulge them, except to those who, after long trial, should be found worthy to succeed them. The Kings even prohibited the revelation of them on pain of death. This secret was styled the Sacerdotal Art, and included alchemy, astrology, magism, the science of spirits, etc. He gave them the key to the Hieroglyphics of all these secret sciences, which were regarded as sacred, and kept concealed in the most secret places of the Temple.*"

These occult concepts - ideas which permeate all of Freemasonry (unbeknownst to most of its members) - are exactly those which the Books of Enoch describe as being taught to man by fallen angels. In fact, it was the very teaching of these things to man which are given as a reason for the fallen angels' condemnation in the first place.

Therefore, you can see that even in the ancient world, the holy was mixed with the unholy, the divine was mixed with the demonic, in order to draw men away from the very truth which these organizations outwardly claimed to teach. It is not for man to study alchemy and magic; it is rather our duty and our goal to turn from such unfruitful teachings and submit to the will of our God instead. These temptations have always existed, and we must decide whether to imitate the acquiescence of Eve or the obedience of Mary.

Without explicitly stating it, the underlying frame of the Masonic Mysteries is that there is no meaningful difference between the Mysteries of any given culture or time; that none is better or worse than any other; that "religious indifference" is the only reasonable position to take. It brings Christ back down to the level of what came before Him; it negates His work and sacrifice; it chips away at the mind of the faithful, implying that all schools of knowledge are somehow "equal."

And yet, in Truth, there is nothing to be offered by the pagan Mysteries in the modern Christian world. There is nothing they prefigured which has not been fulfilled, nothing they once pointed to which has not been completed, and nothing they can do for man which Christ Himself cannot. They are the crumbled pillars of an obsolete building, distant shadows of the fullness of Christ, and serve no purpose in the modern world but to distract from the one and only true path to salvation.

Even what may have once been holy in them has been completely overshadowed by participation in genuine Orthodox Christianity; for as St. John of Kronstadt so accurately pointed out, *"If one were to put all of the world's most precious things on one side of a scale, and the Divine Liturgy on the other, the scale would tip completely in favor of the Liturgy."*

Therefore, do not be fooled by those who conflate truth with lies. Drink no mixture of water and oil, but rather allow nothing impure to approach your lips. Drink only from Christ, the everlasting fountain, and be content to disdain all else. Having become one of us, Christ rendered the pagan

Mysteries unfruitful and worthless; they have nothing whatsoever to add to His teachings.

For Christ gave us Mysteries as well, but of an entirely different nature. As the Orthodox chant in the Resurrectional Theotokion, *"the Mystery which was hidden from everlasting and was unknown of the angels, O Theotokos, wast revealed through thee, to those who dwell upon the earth. In that God, having become incarnate - in unconfused union - of His own good will accepted the Cross for our sake. Whereby He raised again the first created, and hath saved our souls from death."*

St. Paul describes our Mysteries when he writes in **Colossians 1:26** of **"*the mystery that has been kept hidden for ages and generations, but is now disclosed to the Lord's people. To them God has chosen to make known among the Gentiles the glorious riches of this mystery, which is Christ in you, the hope of glory.*"**

The true Christian Mystery, contained within and revealed by the rites of the Orthodox Church, was not like that of the pagans. The great Christian Mystery - the "mega mysterion" - was not known to the angels, to the demons, to the wise, or to the initiated adepts. It was hidden from all creation until the Incarnation of Jesus Christ in the flesh.

Therefore, any Masonic claims as to the "equivalency" of the pagan and Christian mysteries are transparently false and absurd. It is simply gibberish to suggest that the Apostles would secretly be teaching the exact things they were writing against, and any man with a shred of sense knows it.

Lastly, let us examine the physical orientation of Masonic Lodges - as this is also an important piece of the puzzle. Where possible, they are situated East by West, with the chair of the "Worshipful Master" (the administrative head of the Lodge) in the East.

The "front" of each room, or the door through which all new candidates enter a Masonic Lodge for the very first time, is flanked on each side by a pillar. These pillars, which are explained differently depending on the Degree which a man is receiving, are described in the Blue Lodge as "Jachin" and "Boaz" - the Biblical names of the pillars in front of King Solomon's Temple.

During each of his 3 Blue Lodge Degrees, the candidate will stand between these pillars and receive a brief speech about a particular aspect of the fraternity which he is joining. Later on, should he continue to the Scottish Rite, it is revealed to him that these pillars actually represent occult Kabbalistic concepts (the principles of Mercy and Severity).

As we learn in the Holy Scriptures, the shape and form of King Solomon's Temple was based on the Tabernacle in the wilderness. Describing the Temple and its High Priests, St. Paul wrote that **"They serve at a sanctuary that is a copy and shadow of what is in heaven. This is why Moses was warned when he was about to build the tabernacle: 'See to it that you make everything according to the pattern shown you on the mountain.'" (Hebrews 8:5)**

This is likewise how Orthodox Churches are built: as a representation of the Temple and the Tabernacle, themselves a representation of where the angels serve in Heaven. Orthodox Priests serving at the altar are carrying out the same functions, with a similar role and presentation, as the High Priests in King Solomon's Temple.

Masonry has stolen the shape of these divine forms, mimicking what is holy and perverting it for occult purposes.

As you now understand, Masonry is a religion unto itself. It contains mysteries, initiations, language, and sacraments which ape those of the Orthodox Church - while neglecting the name of Christ and spiritually leading in the exact opposite direction. It is a vestigial remnant of ancient pagan cultures, and is utterly irrelevant for modern man's spiritual progress.

It seems, therefore, that in giving Freemasonry to the world, Satan has designed the perfect trap. It draws the honest and well-meaning like moths to a flame…and just like when the moths finally arrive at their destination, there is nothing but destruction in store for its members.

To prove to you that this is the case, let us dive a bit deeper into the Mysteries of both Orthodoxy and Freemasonry, in order to answer the fundamental question which underpins this entire book: *What are people seeking, and what is being offered?*

Pike once described Masonry as "*a struggle towards the Light*"…but as St. Jerome so accurately noted, the heretics *"mean one thing in their heart; they promise another with their lips. They speak with piety and conceal impiety. They speak Christ and hide the Antichrist, for they know that they will never succeed with their seduction if they disclose the Antichrist. They present light only to conceal darkness; through light they lead to darkness."*

As you will understand by the time you're done reading the next chapter, **Light And The Lost Word**, that phrase has a very different meaning for Masons than it does for Christians.

"And no wonder, for Satan himself masquerades as an angel of light."

2 Corinthians 11:14

# LIGHT AND THE LOST WORD

In his commentary on the 4th Degree, *Secret Master*, Pike writes that *"Truth and the Lost Word, which are Light, are within the reach of every man, would he but open his eyes and see."*

All of Freemasonry is thus underpinned by a "search for the Lost Word," which various Masonic Degrees and philosophers have referred to as a "key" which unlocks the secrets of the Universe. From the beginning to the end of a man's Masonic journey, he is said to be in search of this "Light" and "Lost Word," which can only be discovered - so he is told - by studying and applying the lessons of various philosophical systems.

Right away, a true Christian should be struck by the idea that Light and the Word of God are *"lost"* in the eyes of the Masonic fraternity. If the Word is lost, who then is Christ? What did He come to teach us? What, in the eyes of Freemasonry, is there to learn outside of His lessons - and what is the "truth" to which these extra-Christian lessons are supposed to lead?

The Light which Christians seek, and in which Christians dwell, is none other than the Light of Jesus Christ: He who illuminates our minds and hearts, shining into every corner of our souls, that we may know the difference between darkness and The Way. The Light of Christ heals our wounds, suppresses our passions, softens our hearts, enlightens our minds, and gives Life to those parts of us which were previously dead. The Light of Christ restores sight to the blind, hearing to the deaf, feeling to the numb, and love to the bitter.

It is the Light of God's grace which was revealed to the Apostles on Mount Tabor, and is likewise revealed to us in the proper dose which we are prepared to receive. It is the gradual illumination of our lives as we improve in self-denial and self-renunciation, seeking to become empty of our ourselves and more full of Christ. It is dispensed through the sacraments, attends us during reverent and heartfelt prayer, receives our tears when we repent, and defeats the Enemy on our behalf. It is truly the Light which **"shines in the darkness, and the darkness has not overcome it." (John 1:5)**

We know where our Light is, and the method by which to grow in Him. Is this the same "Light" which Masons seek? As you will soon understand, the answer to this question is a resounding "No!"

In some Masonic jurisdictions, new candidates are taught that they have "long lived in darkness" before seeking the "Light" of Masonry. When a man is told he has "long been in darkness," could a Christian accept such a statement?

Is a man who follows Christ "in darkness" until joining the Masonic fraternity? And if so, what does that say about the Nicene Creed - in which we state that Jesus Christ is "*Light of Light?*"

Over and over again throughout Holy Scripture and Holy Tradition, we are taught exactly where to find Light and the Word of God.

Indeed, a Christian believes that **"In the beginning was the Word, and the Word was with God, and the Word was God." (John 1:1)** The Word of God was "*begotten of the Father before all ages,*" and was "*incarnate of the Holy Spirit and the Virgin Mary*" in the Person of Jesus Christ. Our Word is not "lost," but spoke to men face-to-face.

By way of contrast, let us examine what Pike writes about the "Word of God" in his commentary on the 13th Degree, *Royal Arch Of Solomon*. In it, he asserts that *"the true knowledge of God, of His nature and His attributes, is written by Him upon the leaves of the great Book of Universal Nature, and may be read there by all who are endowed with the requisite amount of intellect and intelligence. This knowledge of God, so written there, and of which Masonry has in all ages been the interpreter, is the Master Mason's Word."*

He further states that *"the light of Reason, given by God to man, by which he is enabled to read in the Book of Nature the record of the thought, the revelation of the attributes of the Deity,"* and quotes again from Matter in saying that *"he who has the key of science will interpret all according to the light he possesses."*

Now, it is true that the perfect order and harmony of nature are proof of God's divine thumbprint on the world. Christians can agree that the Word of God is He who ordered the stars, Who separated the seas from land, and Who put everything in the cosmos in its proper place. Why, then, remove the name of Jesus Christ from this equation?

For Pike, Christ is just another in a long line of "Words" which have been revealed throughout the history of religion. In his commentary on the 18th Degree, *Knight Rose Croix*, he quotes from arch-heretic Arius in order to support this assertion:

"*'When God resolved to create the human race,' said Arius, 'He made a Being that He called The WORD, The Son, Wisdom, to the end that this Being might give existence to men.'*"

Pike then adds that *"This WORD is the Ormuzd of Zoroaster, the Ainsoph of the Kabbalah, the Nous of Plato and Philo, the Wisdom or Demiurgos of the Gnostics. That is the True Word, the knowledge of which our ancient brethren sought as the priceless reward of their labors on the Holy Temple."*

As you saw with the previous chapter, a large amount of Masonic energy is dedicated to conflating Christ and Christianity with other figures and religions; if the demon succeeds in its efforts, the Mason is left falsely believing that all religions are fundamentally the same.

Therefore, the Light of transfiguration into Christ's most Holy image is completely alien to the Masonic mind. Instead, it seeks rational and scientific knowledge of the created world, preferring a naturalistic approach to God. We will dive deeper into the failings of this approach in the following chapter.

As you can tell, the purpose of Freemasonry is to send its members on a wild spiritual goose-chase, seeking after something which is simply a distraction from the true Word of God: Jesus Christ. It plants seeds of mystery and fascination in the minds of the unguarded, dangling the carrot of supposed "knowledge" ever before their eyes, leading them through a labyrinth of nothing which ends only in spiritual blackness.

If you do not believe me, search for images of Albert Pike, Manly P. Hall, and J.D. Buck. Look into their eyes, and tell me how much "Light" you see.

Thus, both Freemasons and Christians are engaged in a lifelong search for Light and the Word of God. You have learned that both "Light" and the "Word of God" are defined differently by Masons than they are by Christians, and that Masonic philosophers go to great lengths conflating the two.

As always, Pike wants to spread the **Gnostic** deception that all of the Patriarchs and Prophets secretly believed in the underlying principles of Masonry - rather than what they shared with the world. He writes in his commentary on the 17th Degree, *Knight Of The East And West*, that *"Moses and Aaron, his brother, the whole series of High Priests, the Council of the 70 Elders, Solomon and the entire succession of Prophets, were in possession of a higher science; and of that science Masonry is, at least, the lineal descendant. It was familiarly known as the Knowledge of the Word."*

To Pike, the Word of God is occult scientific knowledge, hidden from the "ignorant" masses through a web of undecipherable symbols - known only to the philosophical elite who are "wise" enough to understand it. It is the same trick, over and over again.

In the following chapter, I will demonstrate to you that all you have learned so far - that Masonry and Christianity are incompatible religions, seeking a different Light and a different Word of God - stems primarily from the differences in what is meant by "God" in the first place.

I will also demonstrate to you the underlying philosophical doctrine from which springs all you have read thus far - especially Masonry's religious indifference and insistence that there is only one "true religion" which underlies all the others.

As you will soon understand, there is no reconciliation between Christian and Masonic **Theology**…so with that in mind, let us continue our journey.

"Do not be yoked together with unbelievers. For what do righteousness and wickedness have in common? Or what fellowship can light have with darkness?"

2 Corinthians 6:14

# THEOLOGY

The simplest way to describe Christian theology is to refer to what we confess and affirm in the Nicene Creed: that we *"believe in One God, the Father Almighty, Maker of Heaven and Earth, and of all things visible and invisible...and in One Lord, Jesus Christ, Son of God, the only-begotten, begotten of the Father before all ages, Light of Light, true God of true God, begotten not created, of one essence with the Father, by Whom all things were made...and in the Holy Spirit, the Lord, the giver of life, Who proceeds from the Father, Who with the Father and the Son together is worshipped and glorified, and Who spoke through the prophets."*

We confess One God in three Persons, the Holy Trinity, distinct yet joined in hypostatic union, one of Whom became man and was crucified and resurrected to save us from corruption and death. Any deviation from this theological formula is inherently un-Christian and, subsequently, cannot and should not be confessed by any man who claims to follow the Christian faith.

As you have already learned, all Masonic candidates must express a belief in a "Supreme Being," sometimes referred to by Masons as the "Great Architect of the Universe." This chapter, therefore, will explore the nature and attributes of this "Great Architect" to see whether it aligns with orthodox Christian theology.

Before we begin this exploration, it must be said that there are certainly Masons who confess the Nicene Creed. You will find good Christian men in many Masonic Lodges who mistakenly believe that Freemasonry is compatible with their faith. You will also find many men who despise Christianity.

Ironically, there are even Masonic occultists who complain that the Lodge has become *too* Christian, despite its wide-ranging efforts to eradicate any semblance of genuine Christianity from its Degrees. This is the group to which I once belonged, and I distinctly remember commiserating with an esoteric friend in Lodge that Masonry "used to teach material of real substance, before all these Christians got here and subdued it!"

It is the theological views of these occult Masons, whom I believe make up the overwhelming majority of Freemasonry's highest offices, which I will be dissecting in this chapter. If you are a Christian Mason reading along, please understand that this is what most of your superiors believe - including the men who designed the Degrees in the first place.

In order to understand the Masonic approach to theology, it is first necessary to understand the various routes by which theology can be approached in the first place. Christian theology, as described above, is the result of *divine revelation*.

It is a theology revealed to men by God Himself, in one or more of His three Persons, in various ways throughout the ages. This revealed theology has been captured and communicated through the Holy Scriptures and the Councils, services, hymns, and iconography of the Orthodox Church.

By way of contrast, and as mentioned briefly earlier, Masonic theology takes a *naturalistic* approach. As you will soon see, Masonry seeks to reason its way to God by a careful study of nature and the faulty logic of the human mind. Christian theology begins in Heaven and works its way down to Earth; Masonic theology begins on Earth and tries to work its way up to Heaven.

Pike makes this abundantly clear in his commentary on the 2nd Degree, *Fellowcraft*. Quoting from Theodore Parker's Ten Sermons Of Religion, he writes that "*Familiarity with the grass and trees, the insects and the infusoria, teaches us deeper lessons of love and faith than we can glean from the writings of Fénelon and Augustine. The great Bible of God is ever open before mankind."*

In his commentary on the following Degree, Pike elaborates to the new Mason that *"For further instruction as to the symbolism of the heavenly bodies, and of the sacred numbers, and of the temple and its details, you must wait patiently until you advance in Masonry, in the mean time exercising your intellect in studying them for yourself. To study and seek to interpret correctly the symbols of the Universe, is the work of the sage and the philosopher. It is to decipher the writing of God, and penetrate into His thoughts."*

Certainly, no Christian would deny that the order and harmony of nature is proof of God's intelligent design. To suggest otherwise would be to assert that a painting can think itself into existence with no painter behind the brush. But that is a far cry from Parker's assertion that the Scriptures and the Saints have less to teach than a blade of grass or the shape of a raindrop.

Perhaps one of the reasons for why Masons study God in this way is to support their non-dogmatic approach to religion as a whole. After all, the same blade of grass can be equally studied by scientists who are Jewish, Christian, Muslim, or Hindu. All will agree on the color of the grass and of what parts it consists, seeing an order to its construction that cannot be random.

But this approach cannot ever lead to a true understanding of the Holy Trinity, which is revealed not by nature but by God Himself. And if any approach to theology does not result in what Christians know to be true, then we cannot count it as valid or spiritually fruitful.

We also believe that God is known through our participation in His divine and uncreated Energies. The less we become like *ourselves* through self-denial and partaking of the Holy Gifts, the more we become like *Him* instead.

We further know God's will because He came in the flesh and explained it to us. He became one of us, in order to show us The Way. The Son modeled perfect obedience to the Father; He demonstrated a life of humility and self-denial; He showed us the meaning of suffering with dignity - and without ever cursing those who caused Him harm.

By way of comparison, Masonry preaches a God so far beyond the capacity of man to comprehend that nothing about Him can truly be known apart from what is taught symbolically in secret mystery rituals. Pike quotes many times from William Greg's Creed Of Christendom, an oddly-named document that appears to have little in common with orthodox Christian beliefs.

In one of the quoted passages, Greg writes on the topic of God that "*The common understanding has no humility. Its God is an incarnate Divinity. Imperfection imposes its own limitations on the Illimitable, and clothes the Inconceivable Spirit of the Universe in forms that come within the grasp of the senses and the intellect, and are derived from that infinite and imperfect nature which is but God's creation. We are all of us, though not all equally, mistaken. The cherished dogmas of each of us are not, as we fondly suppose, the pure truth of God; but simply our own special form of error, our guesses at truth, the refracted and fragmentary rays of light that have fallen upon our own minds. Our little systems have their day, and cease to be; they are but broken lights of God; and He is more than they.*"

Over and over, a Masonic **Theology** emerges in which no system, God, or religion has any more or less truth than another; that each is simply a small piece of the picture shared with a specific people at a specific time by the same God, who taught the same thing time and time again; that the masses have never *truly* understood God, Whose true attributes were known only to a tiny circle of the spiritual and intellectual elite in each age and nation throughout history.

This, of course, is strictly opposed to what the Church has taught from the very beginning: that God became man, showed us The Way, conquered death on our behalf, and has reopened the gates of Paradise to all who would deny ourselves, pick up our Cross, and follow Him. Christ delivered the Gospel once and for all to mankind as a whole; there was no "secret wisdom" needed for salvation which somehow escaped the grasp of the masses.

Greg continues his tirade in asserting that *"if we, of the nineteenth century after Christ, adopt the conceptions of the nineteenth century before Him; if our conceptions of God are those of the ignorant, narrow minded, and vindictive Israelite; then we think worse of God, and have a lower, meaner, and more limited view of His nature, than the faculties which He has bestowed are capable of grasping...What is Truth to the philosopher, would not be Truth, nor have the effect of Truth, to the peasant. The religion of the many must necessarily be more incorrect than that of the refined and reflective few, not so much in its essence as in its forms, not so much in the spiritual idea which lies latent at the bottom of it, as in the symbols and dogmas in which that idea is embodied."*

Pike agrees with the statement by writing that *"God is, as man conceives Him, the reflected image of man himself."* Underlying this philosophy is the notion that somehow, as science and philosophy improve, our understanding of God should improve along with it; that we should throw out "antiquated" notions of Who God Is, as they are apparently made irrelevant by new discoveries and "updated" morality; that somehow, God changes along with our conception of Him.

To a Christian, God has never changed. He does not change now, nor will He ever, for He is the same throughout all ages and is not affected by human knowledge in any way. Our God is "*the same yesterday, today, and forever.*" **(Hebrews 13:8)**

The question then becomes: *If Masons reject Divine Revelation in the form of Holy Scripture and Holy Tradition, what form of Theology <u>do</u> they accept?*

## The Key To All Masonry

The answer to that question is the key to all Masonry; namely, a demonic doctrine known as the Kabbalah. While this system is never openly mentioned during the 3 Degrees of the Blue Lodge (though they are permeated with its concepts), it is explicitly named as Masonry's philosophical underpinning during the 4th Degree of the Scottish Rite, *Secret Master.*

In his commentary on the 3rd Degree, *Master Mason*, Pike does however use a quote from Eliphas Lévi's <u>History Of Magic</u> which neatly summarizes Masonic **Theology.** According to Lévi, a radical Communist and notorious sorcerer, *"Humanity has never really had but one religion and one worship. This universal light has had its uncertain mirages, its deceitful reflections, and its shadows; but always, after the nights of Error, we see it reappear, one and pure like the Sun."*

As is common with the possessed, Pike likewise believed in this "one true religion," which is often called "the secret doctrine" in theosophical and occult books. According to the theory, there is one esoteric philosophy which is the core of every exoteric religion - and any superficial differences between these religions are the result of the ignorant masses failing to properly understand what they've been taught.

Pike writes in <u>Morals And Dogma</u> that *"The primary tradition of the single revelation has been preserved under the name of the 'Kabbalah' by the Priesthood of Israel. The Kabbalistic doctrine, which was also the dogma of the Magi and of Hermes, is contained in the Sepher Yetzirah, the Zohar, and the Talmud."*

This is the **Gnostic** goofiness which Pike spends so much time trying to convince his brethren is the "real meaning" of the Gospel of Jesus Christ - going so far as to say that the Apostles themselves received and communicated it in secret.

Pike writes that *"Among all the ancient nations there was one faith and one idea of Deity for the enlightened, intelligent, and educated, and another for the common people. To this rule the Hebrews were no exception. [God], to the mass of the people was like the gods of the nations around them, except that he was the peculiar God, first of the family of Abraham, of that of Isaac, and of that of Jacob, and afterwards the national God...But such were not the ideas of the intellectual and enlightened few among the Hebrews. It is certain that they possessed a knowledge of the true nature and attributes of God; as the same class of men did among the other nations - Zoroaster, Menou, Confucius, Socrates, and Plato. But their doctrines on this subject were esoteric; they did not communicate them to the people at large, but only to a favored few; and as they were communicated in Egypt and India, in Persia and Phoenicia, in Greece and Samothrace, in the greater mysteries, to the Initiates."*

Quoting again from Lévi, Pike writes that *"The Holy Kabbalah, or tradition of the children of Seth, was carried from Chaldea by Abraham, taught to the Egyptian priesthood by Joseph, recovered and purified by Moses, concealed under symbols in the Bible, revealed by the Saviour to Saint John, and contained, entire, under hieratic figures analogous to those of all antiquity, in the Apocalypse of that Apostle."*

Pike quotes from Lévi's Transcendental Magic several times in his commentary on the 28th Degree, *Knight Of The Sun or Prince Adept*. He writes that *"All truly dogmatic religions have issued from the Kabbalah and return to it: everything scientific and grand in the religious dreams of the illuminati, Jacob Boehme, Swedenborg, Saint-Martin, and others, is borrowed from the Kabbalah; all the Masonic associations owe to it their Secrets and their Symbols....The Bible, with all the allegories it contains, expresses, in an incomplete and veiled manner only, the religious science of the Hebrews. The doctrine of Moses and the Prophets, identical at bottom with that of the ancient Egyptians, also had its outward meaning and its veils. The Hebrew books were written only to recall to memory the traditions; and they were written in Symbols unintelligible to the Profane."*

Pike then asserts that *"This philosophy was concealed by the Alchemists under their Symbols, and in the jargon of a rude Chemistry - a jargon incomprehensible and absurd except to the Initiates; but the key to which is within your reach; and the philosophy, it may be, worth studying."*

Possessed occultists love to speak in this manner, weaving dazzling stories together of how their "secret doctrines" were transmitted down throughout the ages, all without presenting a single shred of evidence to support them. They will look you in the eye and tell you, without blinking, that the Gospel is secretly the exact same thing from which God rescued the Israelites in ancient Egypt.

And what, dare we ask, is the goal of these alchemical secrets which we're told the Apostles secretly knew and taught? Lévi openly admits in Transcendental Magic that *"To be always rich, always young, and never to die: such has been in all times the dream of the Alchemists."*

What business does a Christian have with this nonsense? To be always rich and young? Never to die? Truly, Satan's tactics have never changed.

Lévi may as well be quoting from the serpent in the Garden of Eden, who whispered this lie for the very first time into Eve's unguarded ear: ***"Surely you shall not die."*** **(Genesis 3:4)** It was the lie he told in the beginning, and is the lie he still tells today.

The forms have changed, but the substance has not; Satan does not care whether we call it Kabbalah or Alchemy, so long as it leads us astray.

As with much of what mistakenly passes for "enlightenment" in our New Age society, I suspect that Lévi's thoughts were mostly channeled by him during encounters with dark spirits. Many occultists are "shown" and "taught" things during these experiences - none of which are actually true - but which can appear and feel very convincing at the time.

Once again, we see the spirit of Masonry doing everything within its power to draw the mind of man away from Christ. *Study Kabbalah*, it whispers into the unwary man's ear. *You're so close, you're almost there - it's just within your reach!*

And so the naive man will buy and study books on Kabbalah, on Alchemy, on the so-called "science of Initiation," all the while numbing his soul to the urgings of the Holy Spirit and blinding his mind from seeing the Light of Jesus Christ.

Such nonsense defies both common sense and the Scriptural interpretation passed down to us by the Holy Fathers. It is nothing but a demonic distraction from salvation in Jesus Christ, which cannot be obtained through the Kabbalah or any other system, and is infecting the world today at a rate never before seen in our planet's history.

The Enemy has removed God from schools; he has raised men to positions of prominence as a reward for their attacks on Divine Revelation; he has promoted every kind of filth and baseness across every possible medium of "entertainment;" he has instituted the mass-sacrifice of children and called it a "human right;" he has declared that up is down and black is white. Every possible door has been flung open through which demons may influence mankind, and Satan is ever at work chipping away at the seals which protect us.

Therefore, it should come as no surprise that we find ourselves in the position which we are currently in. Metaphysically speaking, it would be impossible for us *not* to be in this position; the onslaught of demonic and occult influence in our society is the inevitable result of our apostasy from Truth.

Believing in the Kabbalah was an easy error for me to fall into, unguarded by the Holy Spirit and the Orthodox Church which protects us from such demonic influence, specifically because of my own personal weaknesses at the time. I desired more power, more wealth, more influence, more sex; and there was the Kabbalah, offering me a fast and easy path to each. It is through my descent into such grave mistakes, and being rescued from them by Jesus Christ and His holy grace, that I am now able to see so clearly the spiritual potholes into which the unwary fall.

The Enemy can only attack us where we are weak and unguarded. By humility and repentance, we deprive him of the opportunity to lead us astray. And when we cease to lust after power, money, sex, and influence, his tricks are exposed for what they are: utterly powerless against the glory of God.

So if Pike and other Masonic adepts preached the Kabbalah as the only "true" philosophy, what exactly does it teach about God?

In his commentary on the 28th Degree, *Knight Of The Sun or Prince Adept*, Pike neatly summarizes the Kabbalistic view of God in answer to that question. He writes that *"God is the First; indestructible, eternal, uncreated, indivisible...He is silent, and consents with Mind, and is known to Souls through Mind alone. In Him were all things originally contained, and from Him all things were evolved. For out of His Divine Silence and Rest, after an infinitude of time, was unfolded the Word, or the Divine Power; and then in turn the Mighty, ever-acting, measureless Intellect; and from the Word were evolved the myriads of suns and systems that make the Universe."*

While the Biblical God *created* the Universe, the Kabbalistic "God" simply *emanated* it as an extension of Himself. Describing the qualities of the Universe in his commentary on the 31st Degree, *Grand Inspector Inquisitor Commander*, Pike says they *"emanate from one centre and are projected into space, so the whole Universe has emanated from God."*

This is a consistent view of Pike's, who mentions elsewhere that *"According to the Kabbalah, as according to the doctrines of Zoroaster, everything that exists has emanated from a source of infinite light."*

Therefore, Kabbalistic theology teaches that there is nothing in existence which is *not* God. While Orthodox Christians believe that the entire cosmos is sustained by the *Energies* of God, the Kabbalah preaches that every atom of matter is - in some small part - God's *Essence*. The distinction between the Essence and Energies of God is so fundamental to Orthodox theology that it was declared a dogmatic teaching at the Palamite Synods of the 14th century.

Since Scottish Rite Masons are taught that the Kabbalah is they "key to the Mysteries," we will spend the rest of this chapter exploring its various tenets. It should be noted that, despite what Scottish Rite Masons are taught regarding this particular philosophy, very few care enough to bother exploring it themselves. Many Masons are concerned with little more than lapel pins, titles, and collecting Degrees for their "Masonic Resumé" - which the Degrees themselves often chastise as a motivation.

However, without a solid grasp of the Kabbalah, no Mason can begin to comprehend the philosophical lessons which he repeats to his brethren from rote memorization. Any Christian Freemason who truly understood the Kabbalah's perversion of the Christian Trinity, as you will understand momentarily, would be forced to choose on the spot whether to remain in the Lodge or to follow Jesus Christ instead.

As an example, Pike writes in his commentary on the 26th Degree that "*In the Kabbalah, or the Hebrew traditional philosophy, the Infinite Deity, beyond the reach of the Human Intellect, and without Name, Form, or Limitation, was represented as developing Himself, in order to create, and by self-limitation, in ten emanations or out-flowing, called Sephiroth, or rays. The first of these, in the world Atziluth, that is, within the Deity, was Kether, or the Crown, by which we understand the Divine Will or Potency. Next came, as a pair, Hakemah and Bainah, ordinarily translated 'Wisdom' and 'Intelligence,' the former termed the Father, and the latter the Mother. Hakemah is the active Power or Energy of Deity, by which He produces within Himself Intellection or Thinking: and Bainah, the passive Capacity, from which, acted on by the Power, the Intellection flows. This Intellection is called Daath: and it is the "Word" of Plato and the Gnostics; the unuttered word, within the Deity. Here is the origin of the Trinity of the Father, the Mother or Holy Spirit, and the Son or Word.*"

With such elaborate nonsense as the doctrines of the Kabbalah, it is difficult to even know where to start unpacking it. Notice that Pike refers to it as *"the traditional Hebrew philosophy,"* as that lie will be exposed shortly. But before we get there, let us begin with the very foundation of the doctrine.

Since that paragraph likely appears as a bunch of meaningless gibberish, the simple way to understand it is that Pike is describing the creation of the Universe from a Kabbalistic point of view. He is describing, using that system's particular vernacular, how he believes various invisible forces work together in order to create what we experience as material reality.

It is the process by which Kabbalists believe that God pours Himself into created matter, and they usually study it in order to gain more power and control over their lives.

Rather than humbly putting their lives into God's hands, chanting *"Thy Will be done"* and trusting in His beneficence to lead them towards salvation, Kabbalists seek instead of become their *own* "gods" and thereby better control their own circumstances.

It goes without saying that the control they gain is the result of a deal with the Devil, who steals their souls in exchange for demonic power.

Like many of the insights I've shared with you in this book, it's a lesson I unfortunately learned from personal experience.

The view of the Trinity espoused by Pike, of course, is heretical nonsense - but he doesn't stop there. Satan's goal is for man to believe the Holy Trinity is anything *besides* the revealed Christian God, and so any route he can take is put to use. This is exemplified many times throughout <u>Morals</u>

And Dogma, as various perversions of the Trinity are expounded upon at length.

Pike writes elsewhere, quoting from Mallet's Northern Antiquities, that *"The most ancient Trinitarian doctrine on record is that of the Brahmins. The Eternal Supreme Essence, called PARABRAHMA, BRAHM, PARATMA, produced the Universe by self-reflection, and first revealed himself as BRAHMA, the Creating Power, then as VISHNU, the Preserving Power, and lastly as SIVA, the Destroying and Renovating Power; the three Modes in which the Supreme Essence reveals himself in the material Universe."* Pike comments that these *"soon came to be regarded as three distinct Deities. These three Deities they styled the TRIMURTI, or TRIAD."*

By trying to conflate the Christian Trinity with these ancient pagan doctrines, Pike is subtly trying to convince the reader that our Trinity is "nothing new." In his eyes, our Trinity is just "the same old teaching, but worded differently." Of course, a careful look at the above quote will quickly reveal that the Brahmin and Christian views of the Creator are nothing alike. We believe in three Divine Persons; *not* one Person in three different modes, and *not* three different deities. The former is the heresy of Modalism, while the latter is simply polytheism.

In his commentary on the 3rd Degree, *Master Mason*, Pike writes of Christianity that *"Creation is ascribed to the Father, Redemption or Reformation to the Son, and Sanctification or Transformation to the Holy Spirit, answering unto the mathematical laws of Action, Reaction, and Equilibrium."*

Given that no genuine Christian could possibly make such an error, perhaps A.E. Waite was correct in observing that Pike was a man "on whom the spark of Heaven never fell."

Pike further writes that *"the Egyptians arranged their deities in Triads - the Father or the Spirit or the Active Principle or*

*Generative Power; the Mother, or Matter, or the Passive Principle, or the Conceptive Power; and the Son, Issue or Product, the Universe, proceeding from the two other principles. These were Osiris, Isis, and Horus. In the same way, Plato gives us Thought the Father; Primitive Matter the Mother; and Kosmos the World, the Son, the Universe animated by a soul. Triads of the same kind are found in the Kabbalah."*

In each Masonic Degree, there are three objects on the altar. There is a Holy Book of one's own choosing, as well as the Masonic "Square and Compass" (the logo of the fraternity, usually depicted in the United States with a "G" in the center). These three objects are referred to as the "great lights of Masonry," of which Pike writes that *"These three great lights also represent the great mystery of the three principles, of creation, dissolution or destruction, and reproduction or regeneration, consecrated by all creeds in their numerous Trinities."*

You can thus tell there is simply no reconciliation between the Christian and Masonic views of the Holy Trinity, the creation of the Universe, or even what was being taught by the Apostles in the first place.

As I will now demonstrate, the Kabbalah's view of both God and creation completely negates the Gospel as taught in **John 3:16**, that **"*God so loved the world that he gave his one and only Son, that whoever believes in him shall not perish but have eternal life."***

## How Kabbalah Denies The Gospel

In order to show you how Kabbalah fundamentally denies the truths of **John 3:16**, I will first unpack to you its various implications. By doing so, you will quickly see that Kabbalah cannot possibly account for or explain the meaning of St.

John's world-shaking statement on salvation. I will do this by separating said statement into its three constituent parts.

The phrase "**For God so loved the world**," clearly, describes God as a loving, intentional being with positive and paternal feelings towards the creatures He created in His image. In order for God to love the world (which is to say, humankind), then He must be a conscious being with preferences and emotions.

By way of contrast, the "Supreme Being" of the Kabbalah is essentially a neutral, emotionless source of energy that simply *exists* - and then manifests the physical world as an outpouring of *itself*. As you have already seen, Masonic occultists tend to believe that ascribing emotions like love to the eternal God is simply the result of ignorant humans projecting our own qualities onto Him.

Kabbalah mistakes the *clay* for the *potter,* denying the obvious truth that every painting was painted by someone *outside* of it. Not only does each painting have a painter, but it has a painter who chose the colors and the brushstrokes with intention and purpose.

A painting cannot exist just by thinking itself into being. In a similar vein, the Universe does not simply unfold itself according to exact Natural Laws without there being an Author of the same.

By neglecting the painter, the Kabbalistic view of creation - that God is just "source energy" emanating itself into physical form - also removes the idea of a relationship between a painter and his painting.

Therefore, Kabbalah preaches a pantheistic worldview which necessarily removes any notion of *love* from God to humanity. God, in that paradigm, felt no love for the beings which He created; He felt no sadness at their sin, and no desire to bring them back into communion with Him.

This pantheistic "source of energy," which Kabbalists call "Ain Soph Aur" or "limitless light," is the "Universal Mind" of Charles Haanel and "The All" of William Walker Atkinson. Both of these men were occult philosophers, and both of them were Masons.

Furthermore, by bringing God down to the level of humanity and the rest of creation, this pantheistic idea removes the core Gospel message that we need help from *outside of ourselves* in order to be saved.

If God is not separate from humanity and capable of feeling *love* towards us, then the message of **John 3:16** is effectively negated.

After all, why and how could a neutral "source of all that is" send "its Son" to save humanity, if it's all just one big blob differentiated into various parts? The occult concept of the Universe as "one differentiated into many" has more in common with Buddhism or Hinduism than it does with orthodox Christianity.

According to Father Seraphim Rose in his excellent book Orthodoxy And The Religion Of The Future, this is no mere coincidence. I highly recommend his book, if this idea interests you, for more details on the subject.

Therefore, it is easy to conclude that no one who mistakes the creation for the Father - as many New Agers, deceivers, Kabbalists, and Gnostics do - has ever truly known the grace and mercy of Jesus Christ. If they had, it would be impossible to fall into such a mass of theological and soteriological errors.

I say this not out of judgment, but out of sympathy and for a sense of clarity and discernment in spiritual matters. Such individuals should be prayed for, that they may come to know the true and living God. May they turn their backs on the lies of the Devil, and may God treat them with mercy and kindness.

We also read in **John 3:16** that Christ is the "***only Son***" of God. What does Masonry say about this? While we will explore this topic in far greater detail in the next chapter, let us for now simply look at where Christ is mentioned - if at all - in the Degrees of Freemasonry.

While Jesus is never named in the Blue Lodge of Freemasonry, He is mentioned in two specific Masonic Degrees that a man can receive after becoming a Master Mason.

Firstly, Jesus is mentioned during a prayer in the Knights Templar Degree - the highest Degree of the York Rite. In order to receive the Knights Templar Degree, a man must first swear under oath that he will defend the Christian faith.

I was quite excited when I received my Knights Templar Degree, and looked forward to what I assumed would be some kind of operation against the enemies of Christendom.

Although I still considered myself Jewish at the time, I already had an accurate enough view of the world to understand that the enemies of Christendom are the enemies of civilization itself.

Thus, I happily agreed to defend the Christian faith from those who would oppose its values. Instead of meaningful contribution to the clash of civilizations, however, all I got was invitations to dinner cruises and the opportunity to wear expensive costumes. Though Jesus Christ is invoked during the prayers of that particular group, there is exactly zero study of the Gospel to be found within its meetings.

The only other place Jesus is mentioned in Freemasonry is in the 18th Degree of the Scottish Rite, the *Knight Of Rose-Croix.* During the lecture of the Degree, Christ is put on the same level as Mohammad as *"a great reformer of humanity."*

Clearly, it is beyond blasphemous to equate the sinless Christ with the violent barbarian Mohammad. The idea that God has ONE Son, whom He gave for all our sakes, is anathema to the Masonic doctrine of **Perennialism** and its endless efforts not to offend any man of any religious persuasion.

But in those efforts to not offend any religion, Masons end up offending God Himself...for as we read in Holy Scripture, ***"No one who denies the Son has the Father; whoever acknowledges the Son has the Father also."* (1 John 2:23)**

Since there is no point in Freemasonry in which Jesus Christ is unequivocally called the Son of God - at least, not in any meaningful and theologically-correct sense of the term - it is very easy to conclude that Masonic philosophy denies it altogether. For if you will not confess that Christ is Lord, then little else you say or believe matters. It is the cornerstone of our faith, and all who deny it are outside the Ark of Salvation.

Lastly, let us address the final part of **John 3:16, *"that whoever believes in him shall not perish but have eternal life."***

While this topic will be addressed more thoroughly in the chapter on **Soteriology**, the key takeaway from this section is to recall that the Devil does *not* need worship to achieve his ends; he simply needs you not to be in communion with

Jesus Christ. Our Enemy has little concern for which tactic defeats you, so long as one of them does so.

Subsequently, anyone who teaches that there is a way to eternally enjoy Paradise with our Father - without faith in His one and only begotten Son - is acting on behalf of the Enemy by distracting our focus from the truth. It is important for me to once more reiterate that Albert Pike's beliefs are not the beliefs of every Mason, and that there is enormous variety in the personal religious feelings of the fraternity's members.

But once again, I shall also reiterate that certain of his sentiments are commonly-held by the Masonic adepts - those who study occult philosophy and base their worldview on the "secret doctrine" rather than on the Gospel of Jesus Christ.

A common theme amongst the deceived is the Pythagorean notion of the "transmigration of the soul." Describing his own **Gnostic** views according to his research on the topic, Pike asserts that *"The soul...was not a mere conception or abstraction; but a reality including in itself life and thought...It was material; but not brute, inert, inactive, lifeless, motionless, formless lightless matter. It was held to be active, reasoning, thinking; its natural home in the highest regions of the Universe, whence it descended to illuminate, give form ... and whither it unceasingly tends to reascend when and as soon as it can free itself from its connection with that matter. From that substance, the souls of men were formed, and by it alone, uniting with and organizing their bodies, men lived."*

Clearly, Masonry's most influential philosopher believed in both reincarnation and the pre-existence of the soul. Further, he appeared to believe that the soul ascends and descends, in and out of physical matter, in some kind of endless cycle - regardless of a person's faith. Aligning with Masonry's stated belief in the "immortality of the soul" - whether a man gives his life to Christ or not - we find the idea that the soul simply inhabits different forms and bodies as the ages come and go.

In some versions of the theory, a soul can be enfleshed as a human, a fish, a dog, and a cat - all in succession - as some kind of punishment or reward for its behavior in a previous life. This also aligns with what we have studied earlier regarding the **Holy And Unholy Mysteries**, as in some cases being reincarnated as a lower form of life may be seen as the punishment for vice (rather than the Christian view of an eternity in Hell).

The entire Kabbalistic view of the soul is summed up by Pike in saying that the Kabbalists believed "*All souls are originally in the world Aziluth, the Supreme Heaven, abode of God, and of pure and immortal spirits. Those who descend from it without fault of their own, by God's order, are gifted with a divine fire, which preserves them from the contagion of matter, and restores them to Heaven so soon as their mission is ended. Those who descend through their own fault, go from world to world, insensibly losing their love of Divine things, and their self-contemplation; until they reach the world Asiyah, falling by their own weight. This is a pure Platonism, clothed with the images and words peculiar to the Kabbalists.*"

Hidden beneath many layers of symbols and allegory, this is the philosophical foundation of the Scottish Rite of Freemasonry. The Scottish Rite itself openly acknowledges in the 32nd Degree that almost nobody is really paying attention to what is being taught...but it's there for any Mason to observe who truly cares to see it.

Pike continues, "*Thus the secret science and mysterious emblems of initiation were connected with the Heavens, the Spheres, and the Constellations: and this connection must be studied by whomsoever would understand the ancient mind, and be enabled to interpret the allegories, and explore the meaning of the symbols, in which the old sages endeavored to delineate the ideas that struggled within them for utterance."*

This line of thinking, commonly discussed in the ancient pagan worlds, is alien to the teachings of Scripture and the Church. Christians are taught that mankind is created in the image and likeness of God, absent any kind of "descent of the soul" through planetary spheres.

It was the view maintained by the heretic Origen, rightly put in his place by the Blessed St. Augustine of Hippo: "*They say that souls, though not, indeed, parts of God, but created by Him, sinned by abandoning God; that, in proportion to their various sins, they merited different degrees of debasement from heaven to earth, and diverse bodies as prison-houses; and that this is the world, and this the cause of its creation, not the production of good things, but the restraining of evil. Origen is justly blamed for holding this opinion.*"

St. Augustine is not the only Saint in Church history to condemn the doctrine of the pre-existence of the soul - nor the only one to condemn the doctrine of reincarnation which usually accompanies it. In fact, Christian Saints have emphatically denied both the soul's pre-existence, and the possibility of reincarnation, as heresies.

St. John Chrysostom said in his <u>Homilies On John</u> that *"As for doctrines on the soul, there is nothing excessively shameful that they [the disciples of Plato and Pythagoras] have left unsaid, asserting that the souls of men become flies and gnats and bushes and that God himself is a [similar] soul, with some other like indecencies. . . . At one time he says that the soul is of the substance of God; at another, after having exalted it thus immoderately and impiously, he exceeds again in a different way, and treats it with insult,* making it pass into swine and asses and other animals of yet less esteem than these."

St. Basil the Great said in <u>The Six Days' Work</u> to *"Avoid the nonsense of those arrogant philosophers who do not blush to liken their soul to that of a dog, who say that they have themselves formerly been women, shrubs, or fish. Have they ever been fish? I do not know, but I do not fear to affirm that in their writings they show less sense than fish."*

Thus, it is clear that these pagan concepts are absolutely foreign to Christian theology. Alas, since Pike spends such an enormous amount of time and effort both attacking the notion of objective Truth and belittling the wisdom of the Christian masses, he likewise seeks to plant these notions in the fertile soil of unguarded minds.

Since Masonry derives its theology from nature and Kabbalistic philosophy instead of from Divine Revelation, it also fundamentally rejects the Christian belief in a pre-Fall Paradise and a post-Fall disaster. As such, Pike cannot seem to fathom the difference between the world as God initially created it and the world as it exists today. He was confused by the state of things in this fallen existence, trying - and failing - to rationalize why God would have designed such a nightmare for His beloved creations.

This sentiment is best illustrated by a passage in his commentary on the 11th Degree, *Sublime Elect Of The Twelve or Prince Ameth*. In it, he writes that *"For though we do not know why God, being infinitely merciful as well as wise, has so ordered it, it seems to be unquestioningly His law, that even in civilized and Christian countries, the large mass of the population shall be fortunate, if, during their whole life, from infancy to old age, in health and sickness, they have enough of the commonest and coarsest good to keep themselves and their children from the continual gnawing of hunger - enough of the commonest and coarsest clothing to protect themselves and their little ones from indecent exposure and the bitter cold; and if they have over their heads the rudest shelter. And He seems to have enacted this law - which no human community has yet found the means to abrogate - that when a country becomes populous, capital shall concentrate in the hands of a limited number of persons, and labor become more and more at its mercy, until mere manual labor, that of the weaver and ironworker, and other artisans, eventually ceases to be worth more than a bare subsistence, and often, in great cities and vast extents of country, not even that, and goes or crawls about in rags, begging, and starving for want of work."*

While I share Pike's sadness upon observing the consequences of our Fall from Paradise, I of course would never dare to accuse God of deliberately creating such conditions for us in the first place. The Fathers have written at length upon the initial state of man: upon his communion with God, upon his spiritual abilities, upon the condition of his body, and upon the perfect harmony with nature and God in which he once existed. The patristic mindset on these topics is explained phenomenally well in an essay by Hieromonk Damascene, titled <u>Created In Incorruption</u>, which was published in a 2008 edition of the *Orthodox Word* magazine.

It is the goal of the Orthodox life to regain as much of this initial state as possible while in the flesh, knowing that none of us will see the completion of the task until after the General Resurrection and the deification of the cosmos as a whole. We understand that our present dying world was never the intention of a cruel and merciless God who feels indifferent towards humanity's suffering, but is rather the consequence of our disobedience towards a just and loving Creator. It is His justice and love which allow us to seek communion and theosis in the first place, drawing us upwards and away from the death and corruption which surround us on all sides.

Pike, however, is puzzled by the present state of affairs - a natural consequence of his disbelief in the Scriptures and their interpretation by the Fathers of our faith. Since he does not believe in the Christian God or the Biblical account of creation and redemption, Pike places salvation onto his own shoulders instead. The Masonic Crusade to heal the world is, fundamentally, a symptom of their disbelief in God's plan for mankind. We are of course called to aid and assist our neighbors in distress; we do not, however, believe that the world can be "fixed" solely through human effort.

As you have now learned, it is *knowledge of the Kabbalah* which is the supposed "light of Masonry." It has nothing whatsoever to do with Christianity, and is opposed to it in every conceivable way. It's a different and incompatible view of the creation, of the Fall, of God, and of His relationship to humanity.

The whole purpose of the **Gnostic** Kabbalah is to trap the mind in a labyrinth which leads farther and farther away from true knowledge of God, Who is made known to us by divine revelation and the transformation we undergo as we draw nearer to Him by a life of repentance and prayer. By dying to ourselves and seeking to become like Him, we learn about His traits and take them on to the best of our faulty and limited ability. We come to know God by seeing our own sins and by comparing what we discover within to the endless grace and mercy which He shows to the repentant sinner, highlighting His boundless forgiveness and our own hard-hearted wrath by contrast.

We learn about God through relationship with Him, through communion with Him, through the Holy Scriptures and Holy Traditions as revealed to the Apostles, and through the divine utterances of the Holy Spirit through the Prophets.

God is not a puzzle to be analyzed; He is a mystery to be approached with fear, with love, with reverence, and with awe.

As a final point on the Kabbalah, recall that Pike and Lévi both taught that it was the *"Hebrew traditional philosophy,"* citing such works as the Talmud and Zohar as "proof." The oral teaching of the Rabbis, as recorded in the Talmud, are precisely what Christ chastised the Pharisees for following in **Mark 7:8**. In that verse, He rebukes them by saying **"You have disregarded the commandment of God to keep the tradition of men."**

Therefore, it should be obvious that the Kabbalah is *not* the *"Hebrew traditional philosophy"* at all. It was more likely developed during the Babylonian exile, and is a combination of these false Rabbinic traditions with the occult and esoteric sciences taught in the Babylonian Mystery Schools. My personal suspicion is that some of the Jews in captivity were initiated into these Mystery Schools, then added the history and imagery of the people of Israel in order to make the doctrines less Chaldean and more Jewish.

As for the Zohar, it is widely-known that the book was a money-making hoax by its 13th-century author, Moshe de Leon, who clearly "channeled" the material from demons and then used it to accrue power and wealth.

In some circles the book's authorship is attributed to "Shimon Bar Yochai," but according to the *Jewish Encyclopedia,* *"There is a story told about how after the death of Moses de Leon, a rich man of Avila named Joseph offered the widow, who had been left without means, a large sum of money for the original from which her husband had made the copy; and she then confessed that her husband himself was the author of the work. She had asked him several times, she said, why he had chosen to credit his own teachings to another, and he had always answered that doctrines put into the mouth of the miracle-working Simeon ben Yohai would be a rich source of profit."*

In a certain sense, it was the progenitor to the modern phenomenon of New Thought philosophy and - even more recently - "The Secret" and the Law of Attraction. Study of the Zohar and its occult Kabbalistic philosophy was initially forbidden by the Sephardic Jews, but rose to prominence in the Jewish community when the balance of power shifted to the Ashkenazi.

If you are not satisfied with Kabbalah, however, Pike has one last heresy to offer. He quotes at length from Augustus Neander's <u>History Of The Christian Religion</u>, presenting certain comments on Gnosticism as if they are worthy of study and reflection.

Pike cites his work in saying that *"In one respect all the Gnostics agreed: they all held that there was a world purely emanating out of the vital development of God, a creation evolved directly out of the Divine Essence, far exalted above any outward creation produced by God's plastic power, and conditioned by preexisting matter. They agreed in holding that the framer of this lower world was not the Father of that higher world of emanation; but the Demiurge, a being of a kindred nature with the Universe framed and governed by him, and far inferior to that higher system and the Father of it...The mass of the Jews, they held, recognized not the angel, by whom, in all the Theophanies of the Old Testament, God revealed Himself; they knew not the Demiurge in his true relation to the Supreme God, who never reveals himself in the sensible world. They confounded the type and the archetype, the symbol and the idea. They rose no higher than the Demiurge; they took him to be the Supreme God Himself. But the spiritual men among them, on the contrary, clearly perceived, or at least divined, the ideas veiled under Judaism; they rose beyond the Demiurge, to a knowledge of the Supreme God; and are therefore properly His worshippers."*

Christianity does not hold that there is a "higher and lower God," one that created a "world of emanation" and another, beneath the first, that created the material world. We believe in One God, the *"Maker of Heaven and Earth"* as already mentioned in the Nicene Creed. Though Neander himself did not have any specific agenda in relating the history of early Christian Gnosticism, Pike's inclusion of these passages - with no subsequent condemnation of them - demonstrate his own intentions rather clearly.

It should be noted that the idea of a Demiurge is not inherently alien to Christianity, as it simply refers to a divine *"maker"* or Creator. However, throughout the history of Christianity, it is usually used by the Gnostics to denote the "lower" of their two "gods" and not used in the proper Christian sense. Some Gnostics held to a beneficent Demiurge, while others perceived him as being hostile to the "Supreme God" who they believed to be good.

Both views are wrong, and neither is compatible with Christianity. There is no route overlooked by the demons in Pike's mind in their relentless assault on the Truth - or their efforts to sway man from focusing on the only true means of salvation.

You have now learned that Masonry is a Mystery Religion which imitates the forms and sacraments of Orthodox Christianity. You have learned that it leads its members to seek a false "Light" and a Word which they falsely proclaim to be "lost." You have learned that it denies the God of the Bible in favor of the impersonal Kabbalistic "deity," and that its views on the Father are strictly at odds with those confessed by all genuine Christians.

You have learned that it teaches a false version of the origin of the soul, the heretical Pythagorean doctrines of transmigration and reincarnation, and that many deny Paradise and our fall from it in the first place. And most importantly, you have learned that very, very few Masons have any idea what goes on in the philosophy of the higher ranks at all.

As I said earlier, to believe that Christianity is compatible with Freemasonry is to be ignorant of both systems. I hope that what you have read thus far has helped convince you that this is the case…and if you are a Mason, that it has gotten you to take a closer look at what is going on around you in Lodge.

If you choose to leave the Lodge after realizing you cannot fully embrace both Masonry and Jesus Christ, then know with confidence that you will not be the first to do so.

With all this in mind, let us explore the question which logically follows from this chapter's material: *If that's the Masonic view of the Father, what's the Masonic view of the Son?*

"See to it that no one takes you captive through hollow and deceptive philosophy, which depends on human tradition and the elemental spiritual forces of this world rather than on Christ."

Colossians 2:8

# CHRISTOLOGY

At its simplest, the field of **Christology** seeks to answer just one question: *Who is Christ?* As we say in the Nicene Creed, Orthodox Christians believe that Jesus Christ is *"the only-begotten Son of God, Light of Light, true God of true God."*

The First Council of Nicaea (in 325) dogmatically defined that Christ is *"of one essence with the Father,"* refuting the Arian heretics who claimed that He was a created being of a lower order. At the Council of Chalcedon in 451, the Person of Jesus Christ was defined as fully-God and fully-human, with both a divine and a human will, combined in one nature via hypostatic union.

At one point or another in Church history, every possible perspective on the nature of Jesus has been discussed, dissected, defined, and declared to be either correct belief (orthodox) or heresy (heterodox). Orthodox Christians, Roman Catholics, and most mainstream Protestants uphold the dogmatic truths about the Person of Jesus Christ - as revealed by the Holy Spirit - in the great Ecumenical Councils.

And yet, despite the hard work of the Apostles and their students letting us know who Christ is...and just as importantly, who Christ is *not*...there is a never-ending stream of heresies and lies with which we must contend.

Freemasonry claims not to be in conflict with any religion, preferring to present itself as being equally respecting and tolerant towards all. And yet, is it truly possible to respect the beliefs of a Christian if one's Christology is not in line with Orthodoxy?

You saw briefly, in the last chapter, that the divinity of Christ in inherently denied through Masonry's general silence on the topic. In this chapter, you will be exposed to some of the more particular Christologies of the occult philosophers who have had such a profound impact on American Freemasonry.

I do not claim that all (or even most) Freemasons would agree with the views you are about to read. In fact, many Freemasons - who are professing Christians - would agree with orthodox Christology.

Instead, I claim that these are the kinds of views typically held by those held in particularly high renown within the fraternity. The visible leadership of the Lodge does not always represent what the true leadership believes, and it is my personal opinion that the doctrines of the occult philosophers carry more weight in Masonry than whatever Christology is maintained by the Masonic "laity."

Even within the occult circles of Masonry, there is a variety of opinions on who Christ is - or in some cases, what He represents. To best illustrate this phenomenon, I have chosen to focus primarily on the Christology of three prominent and influential Masonic occultists: Albert Pike, J.D. Buck, and Manly P. Hall.

As you read this chapter, please recall from the **Spiritual Warfare** section of this book that the 4 Satanic Deceptions in Masonry are **Perennialism**, **Salvation Without Christ**, **Distortion and Perversion**, and **Gnosticism**.

The occult philosophers of Masonry use these 4 Deceptions in a limited - but very persistent - set of ways.

Sometimes, they state plainly that the Gospel of the New Testament does not accurately represent the life and teachings of Jesus Christ.

This **Gnosticism** is the foot-in-the-door which then allows them to insert their own (false) teachings about Christ into the mind of the unwary reader.

Before the Devil can convince you that he is the only "god" worth following, he must first get you to accept certain smaller falsehoods and distortions along the way. Indeed, Satan deceives by degrees.

He gets you to accept first a small lie, and then a bigger one, and then one even larger, in a chain that never ends. Not only does it work slowly and subtly, but the victim's willful compliance seems to be required each and every step of the way.

This concept has been immortalized in film by that classic scene of a vampire arriving at the doorstep of a house. He may only enter a home into which he has been invited, as the Devil is powerless to invade without the victim's consent.

Before a man becomes a Mason, he is first asked: "*Is this of your own free will and accord?*" Answering "yes," in retrospect, is perhaps a Mason's first acceptance of the vampire's wicked desires.

Other times, these philosophers preach **Perennialism** by claiming that Christ is just one of many "dying God-men" throughout time, worthy of no more respect or recognition than "all those who came before."

After all, if there were many "dying God-men" in different cultures throughout time, then there would be no particular reason to follow a specific one over any other.

Thirdly, these men sometimes quote Church Fathers whose writings they claim provide evidence for their points. Some of these quotes, as you will soon discover, are a complete **Distortion and Perversion** of their original meaning.

Other times, they appear to be completely made-up.

I have conducted a thorough search trying to find the origins of certain of these quotes, and I cannot find them in the actual writings of *any* Church Fathers whatsoever.

They do not appear to exist outside of occult literature, but are simply passed from one liar to another for use in their own false and heretical teachings.

Sometimes, they will use genuine Church Father quotes… but either misrepresent the points they were making, or leave out parts which completely demolish their arguments.

In other words, they are lying.

Lastly, these men often state that either "good works lead to immortality" - **Salvation Without Christ** - or that the soul goes to Heaven regardless of anything the person does or believes on Earth.

It is not for nothing that Jesus calls the Devil "***the father of lies!***" **(John 8:44)**

In order to relay to you the importance and influence of each of these 3 men, I will begin each section with an explanation of who they are and why they matter.

Then, I will simply go through their publicly-available writings and quote them to you. We will begin our journey with the views of Albert Pike.

## Pike's Christology

As mentioned earlier, the official position of the Scottish Rite is that Albert Pike was a lifelong Trinitarian Christian. However, you have also seen that Pike's ideas of both Christ and the Trinity more regularly align with those of **Gnostics** and pagans than they do with the Holy Fathers of the Orthodox faith. Lastly, you have seen that he valued his own opinion on the topic at *least* as highly as those of the Saints.

I have read several of Pike's books, and he does not appear to have a very consistent set of beliefs over time. Perhaps he changed his mind often (or perhaps his mind was simply a mesh of too many thoughts to untangle), but his various books are often so different in content and tone that they can sound as though they were written by different men.

Regardless, and despite his many philosophical and theological failings, it does appear that Pike at least believed that a man named Jesus Christ existed and walked upon the Earth.

He writes in Morals And Dogma that "*Above all the other great teachers of morality and virtue, [Masonry] reveres the character of the Great Master Who, submissive to the will of His and Our Father, died upon the Cross. All must admit, that if the world were filled with beings like Him, the great ills of society would be at once relieved. For all coercion, injury, selfishness, and revenge, and all the wrongs and the greatest sufferings of life, would disappear at once. These human years would be happy; and the eternal ages would roll on in brightness and beauty; and the still, sad music of Humanity, that sounds through the world, now in the accents of grief, and now in pensive melancholy, would change to anthems, sounding to the March of Time, and bursting out from the heart of the world.*"

This is a beautiful passage with which all true Christians can easily agree. One time within Morals And Dogma's 971 pages, he even goes so far as to refer to Christ as "God." Indeed, it is true that Pike does not seem to have a higher reverence for any other religious figure than Jesus Christ.

He writes elsewhere in <u>Morals And Dogma</u> that *"Whatever higher attributes the Founder of the Christian Faith may, in our belief, have had or not had, none can deny that He taught and practised a pure and elevated morality, even at the risk and to the ultimate loss of His life. He was not only the benefactor of a disinherited people, but a model for mankind...However the Mason may believe as to creeds, and churches, and miracles, and missions from Heaven, he must admit that the Life and character of Him who taught in Galilee, and fragments of Whose teachings have come down to us, are worthy of all imitation...Divine or human, inspired or only a reforming Essene, it must be agreed that His teachings are far nobler, far purer, far less alloyed with error and imperfection, far less of the earthly, than those of Socrates, Plato, Seneca, or Mahomet, or any other of the great moralists and Reformers of the world."*

Thus, as you can see from the way he tries to "make room" for other teachers and belief systems in his own personal view of Christ, it appears that Pike's zeal for Christianity was not matched by his faith in its exclusive nature.

Despite his professed love of Christ, Pike made many other comments throughout his life which give a *very* different window into what he believed the truth of Christianity actually is. It's possible he just changed his mind on certain topics over time, and equally possible that he was sometimes writing under the influence of various spirits he had "picked up" in his studies of the world's pagan philosophies.

While he clearly had a respect for Christ, he far more often quotes from heretics and **Gnostics** than he does the Gospel or Church Fathers. For example, Pike quotes from Basilides, to whom he refers as *"the first important Christian Gnostic,"* by way of once again citing Matter's book <u>Critical History Of Gnosticism</u>.

Matter writes that *"the Nous united itself, by baptism in the river Jordan, with the man Jesus, servant of the human race; but did not suffer with Him; and the disciples of Basilides taught that the Nous, put on the appearance only of humanity, and that Simon of Cyrene was crucified in His stead and ascended into Heaven."*

This absurd doctrine, heretical in every sense of the word, was refuted by St. Irenaeus in his famous work <u>Against Heresies</u> - and is here reiterated by Pike to warp the minds of the Faithful.

Pike then informs us, again through Matter, that *"The opinion of the [Docetists] as to the human nature of Jesus Christ, was that most generally received among the Gnostics. They deemed the intelligences of the Superior World too pure and too much the antagonists of matter, to be willing to unite with it: and held that Christ, an Intelligence of the first rank, in appearing upon the earth, did not become confounded with matter, but took upon Himself only the appearance of a body, or at the most used it only as an envelope."*

This is the same heresy which St. John the Evangelist spent so much time and energy refuting in his Gospel account and letters, and for a very important reason: If Christ did not take flesh - if He did not become man, in every sense of the word, while also fully maintaining His divine nature - then human beings cannot be regenerated or saved. This is why St. John went to such great lengths emphasizing that **"the Word became flesh, and dwelt among us." (John 1:14)**

His taking on flesh for us, His condescending to enter into the material world of space and time in undivided hypostatic union between God and man, is precisely the mechanism by which matter can be deified and restored to its original state of holiness. For a more complete examination of this topic, I recommend <u>On The Incarnation</u> by St. Athanasius.

Asserting that matter was "too dirty" for Christ to touch is to say that God did not create the world and see **"all that He had made, and it was very good," (Genesis 1:31)** or that God disdained His own creation too much to become like one of us. But it was precisely His Incarnation which allowed Him to die and be resurrected, conquering death on our behalf and reopening the Gates of Paradise from which we had long been barred.

Without ever explicitly agreeing with the various **Gnostic** views on Christology in Morals In Dogma, Pike tends to list them off without ever saying they are wrong. It seems likely that, given his own particular views on the subjective nature of religious truth in the first place, he may have somehow believed that each possible view of Christ was equally valid - provided that whoever holds such a view does so sincerely.

But as we know, religious Truth is not a matter of personal opinion. It is a matter of Who God is, Who He *told us* He is, and Who the Church has maintained He is from the very beginning of Christian history.

Hard as it may be to believe, Pike's Christology was actually the highest (and least offensive) amongst the most famous Masonic adepts. As you will see in a moment, other influential 33rd Degree Scottish Rite Masons had far more blasphemous and obscene opinions.

## Hall's Christology

Manly P. Hall, while he lived, was a prolific lecturer and philosopher who published over 150 books and founded the Philosophical Research Society in 1934. He spent most of his life studying various occult mysteries from all ages and cultures around the world, and was granted the 33rd Degree by the Scottish Rite of Freemasonry for his work in the field.

The 33rd Degree of the Scottish Rite is an invitation-only honor, and so exclusive that asking to receive it...even if you're a 32nd Degree Scottish Rite Mason when you ask... automatically bans you from it for life.

Thus, receiving such a coveted honor means that those in the higher echelons of the institution saw something special and profound about his work. With that in mind, Hall was far from silent on the topic of Christianity.

As with all possessed individuals, the spirits infesting his consciousness took it upon themselves to denigrate, pervert, and distort the Gospel when given the opportunity and platform to do so. If the Masonic fraternity had a problem with Hall's thoughts on the topic of Christ and the Apostles, it is highly unlikely he would have been granted such high honors. So with that being said, let's now examine his writings to see what he believed and taught about Jesus Christ.

The quotes you are about to read come from his most well-known book, called <u>The Secret Teachings Of All Ages: An Encyclopedic Outline Of Masonic, Hermetic, Qabbalistic And Rosicrucian Symbolical Philosophy</u>. It is considered one of the greatest modern works of occult philosophy.

Its second subtitle is, "<u>Being An Interpretation Of The Secret Teachings Concealed Within The Rituals, Allegories, And Mysteries of All Ages</u>." This second subtitle, clearly, is framed in a way which makes it sound certain that all religions and doctrines have the same teaching at their core. As you have already learned, it is common amongst the adepts to promote the Kabbalah as this "secret teaching."

The title and subtitle are written with such authoritative and fanciful language that it's sure to captivate the minds of those who are not spiritually defended against such tricks.

By way of the subtitle alone, Hall is already negating the exclusive nature of the Christian Gospel.

And we're not even on the first page yet!

His chapter on Christ opens with the line, "*The true story of the life of Jesus of Nazareth has never been unfolded to the world, either in the accepted Gospels or in the Apocrypha, although a few stray hints may be found in some of the commentaries written by ante-Nicene Fathers.*"

In the very first line, Hall demonstrates one of the Enemy's 4 major tactics - **Gnosticism**. He wishes you to believe there is "*secret knowledge*" unavailable to your average person, which only these magical occultists have somehow learned.

There is no reason to believe that "*the true story of the life of Jesus of Nazareth*" is unknown, nor any reason to believe that if it *were* unknown, somehow Hall alone would possess this mysterious truth. As read in **John 18:20**, our Lord said that He "***spoke plainly to the world***" and "***said nothing in secret.***"

The sole purpose of Hall's claim is to make unwary readers believe that Christ did not die on the Cross for our salvation. As such, it directly implies that the story in the Gospels is false…and if the Gospels are false, then there is no reason to have faith in Christ. See how demonic logic works?

Shortly afterwards, he makes an attempt at **Perennialism** by quoting from the writings of St. Justin Martyr. However, he twists their meaning and completely ignores their context.

He quotes Martyr as writing, "*And when we say also that the Word, who is the first-birth of God, was produced without sexual union, and that He, Jesus Christ, Our Teacher, was crucified and died, and rose again, and ascended into heaven, we propound nothing different from what you believe regarding those who you esteem sons of Zeus...And if we assert that the Word of God was born of God in a peculiar manner, different from ordinary generation, let this, as said above, be no extraordinary thing to you, who say that Mercury is the angelic word of God."*

Hall thus concludes, speaking again in his own voice, *"From this it is evident that the first missionaries of the Christian Church were far more willing to admit the similarities of their faith and the faiths of the pagans than were their successors in later centuries."*

Hence, he is trying to convince the reader of his book that not only was Jesus Christ essentially no different from what the pagans already believed, but that this insanity was somehow accepted and preached by the early Christian Church. We have already covered the similarities between the **Holy And Unholy Mysteries**, and it has been demonstrated to you that they were emphatically *not* identical.

Martyr was explaining to the Greeks, in this particular defense of Christianity, that the "gods" they'd been worshipping had some similar characteristics to the story of Jesus Christ. The reason for these similarities, Martyr suggested, was because the demons heard the Old Testament prophecies and tried to create fake second-rate copies of the coming Messiah.

Demons know the Scriptures better than most people do...and foreseeing the coming of Christ, could easily create false Christ-like figures to draw attention away from the true Messiah. That is the point St. Justin was making, and which I agreed with earlier as one of the possible reasons to explain Christian and pagan parallels.

Hence, Hall uses Martyr's words in order to defend the exact point Martyr was writing them against!

As I mentioned in the very beginning of this book, I find it very interesting that the same lies appearing on the world stage today have been around since the beginning. Very little has changed in all that time...though I suppose it is unsurprising, given that the demons telling these lies are far older than humanity. They were around before us, and know every trick and piece of bait that humans are likely to fall for.

Read the following passage from Hall, and you will understand why I say that these Masonic authors also simply invent quotes and then attribute them to sources which do not actually exist.

*"In his <u>Secret Sects of Syria and Lebanon</u>, Bernard H. Springett, a Masonic author, quotes from an early book, the name of which he was not at liberty to disclose because of its connection with the ritual of a sect. The last part of his quotation is germane to the subject at hand: 'But Jehovah prospered the seed of the Essenians, in holiness and love, for many generations. Then came the chief of the angels, according to the commandment of GOD, to raise up an heir to the Voice of Jehovah. And, in four generations more, an heir was born, and named Joshua, and he was the child of Joseph and Mara, devout worshippers of Jehovah, who stood aloof from all other people save the Essenians. And this Joshua, in Nazareth, reestablished Jehovah, and restored many of the lost rites and ceremonies. In the thirty-sixth year of his age he was stoned to death in Jerusalem.'"*

The purpose of this passage is to imply that Jesus did not die on the Cross or simply preach with God's power and spirit. Instead, he was "*stoned to death*" and "*restored many of the lost rites and ceremonies.*"

Hall's evidence for this assertion? A book which cannot be named, read, or checked as to its authenticity. It is not difficult to imagine that such a book may not even exist at all.

But the damage has been done, as this unnamed source gives an air of mystery and fascination to Hall's baseless assertion. As mentioned elsewhere, the Devil often seduces by mystery and fascination.

Hall's book continues to grasp at straws and draw tenuous connections between unrelated ideas, ultimately culminating in the same conclusion that *many* deceived **Gnostics** end up teaching: that Christ was simply here to teach you that "you are God."

He writes "*That the Christos represents the solar power reverenced by every nation of antiquity cannot be controverted. If Jesus revealed the nature of purpose of this solar power under the name and personality of Christos, thereby giving to this abstract power the attributes of a god-man, He but followed a precedent set by all previous World-Teachers. This god-man, thus endowed with all the qualities of Deity, signifies the latent divinity in every man. Mortal man achieves deification only through at-one-ment with this divine Self. Union with the immortal Self constitutes immortality, and he who finds his true Self is therefore 'saved.'*"

Hall's trickery grows more elaborate with each passing sentence, does it not? The above passage makes full use of all 4 of the Enemy's tactics: **Perennialism, Salvation Without Christ, Distortion and Perversion, and Gnosticism** are all on full display.

Each of these tricks was warned about by Prophets in both the Old and New Testaments, and the particular heresy and dangers of the "*you are God*" teaching were written about even in the days of Isaiah as he prophesied the fall of Babylon.

He writes in **Isaiah 47:10-11** that "***Your wisdom and knowledge mislead you when you say to yourself, 'I am,***

***and there is none besides me.' Disaster will come upon you, and you will not know how to conjure it away. A calamity will fall upon you that you cannot ward off with a ransom; a catastrophe you cannot foresee will suddenly come upon you."***

Knowing precisely what the demons would later say in their eternal jealousy of man's hope at salvation, this Prophet of God warned even in antiquity of exactly what form their lies would take. For his sickening deception, Hall was granted Freemasonry's highest and most coveted honor.

He then tries to convince the unwary reader that the Cross is simply a typical pagan symbol with no special meaning for Christians.

He writes that "*Many nations deeply considered the astronomical aspect of religion, and it is probable that the Persians, Greeks, and Hindus looked upon the cross as a symbol of the equinoxes and the solstices, in the belief that at certain seasons of the year the sun was symbolically crucified upon these imaginary celestial angles.*"

Whenever Hall wants to convince you of something for which he has no actual evidence, he defaults to phrases such as "it is probable," "rumors have it," "some say," or "according to the wise men." In each case, all he is truly communicating is that he does not know, but wishes to make it sound as if his statements have some kind of meaningful authority.

He continues by writing that "*The fact that so many nations have regarded their Savior as a personification of the sun globe is convincing evidence that the cross must exist as an astronomical element in pagan allegory...There are four basic elements (according to both ancient philosophy and modern science), and the ancients represented them by the four arms of the cross, placing at the end of each arm a*

*Kabbalistic creature to symbolize the power of one of these elements."*

Thus, you can see that Hall is engaging in **Distortion and Perversion** once more in order to draw the mind's attention away from the sacrifice of our Savior upon the Cross. Instead, he wants you to place that attention on elemental spiritual forces.

It is likely this particular lie was already popular even at the time of the Apostles. St. Paul warned his fellow Christians to **"See that no one takes you captive through hollow and deceptive philosophy, which relies on human tradition and the elemental spiritual forces which govern this world, rather than on Christ." (Colossians 2:8)**

The demons are not inventive or creative. Their success relies entirely on a person's lack of true faith and wisdom, and this is why the same tricks come up again and again throughout time. They do not *need* anything new - besides new targets to play tricks on.

Protected by the Church, the Ark of Salvation, it is impossible to be deceived by such transparent and obvious tricks. Thousands of years of defending the faith has left the Enemy powerless against us.

Looking back on these passages now, I am awestruck at how naive I once was.

I am equally grateful for the work the Lord has performed in my heart and mind, pulling me out of such filth and darkness despite my doing nothing to deserve being rescued. Truly, I was unworthy of the grace the Lord bestowed upon me.

Speaking of filth and darkness, let us move onto our final villain: a man by the name of J.D. Buck.

## Buck's Christology

According to his obituary in the Masonic journal *The Builder*, *"Dr. Buck was an active and influential member of every Rite of our historic Order, holding the highest rank both in the esteem of his Brethren and in the gift of the fraternity - including the honorary Thirty-Third Degree of the Scottish Rite in its Northern Jurisdiction. Indeed, he was a recognized leader of a definite school of Masonic thought and propaganda; and while we have never been able to agree with all the conclusions of the school which he represented, we are none the less appreciative of its services to the Craft - knowing that Truth is larger than the formula of any one school or of all schools put together."*

I hope by now it is clear that I do not hate the Freemasons. I am not accusing them of all being devil-worshippers or blasphemers; I am saying that the *spirit of Masonry itself* opposes the Holy Spirit of God. It does what it can to spread anti-Christian sentiments to those of its members who are receptive to such ideas, and J.D. Buck was simply a useful vehicle for its propaganda.

Buck was also a high-ranking member of the Theosophical Society, an occult organization founded by Helena Blavatsky and a small group of others. Its core belief was that which has already been mentioned; that *all* religions stem from the same source, which Blavatsky was responsible for naming the "Secret Doctrine" in her book by that name in 1888.

Despite the inability of any esoteric philosopher to point out a single shred of meaningful evidence to support this theory, it is very pervasive throughout many modern occult and **Gnostic** circles. It is a demonic one-world doctrine, of the kind despised by God since the destruction of Babel's tower.

My resource for this chapter is Buck's book The Symbolism of Freemasonry (also called Mystic Masonry). While I was still deceived, I used to take quotes from this book - the very same quotes I will soon write out to you as I debunk them - and post them on a Facebook page which I specifically created to help spread occult Masonic teachings.

As you can tell from Hall's diminishing the Cross in the previous section, the **Distortion And Perversion** of symbols is an important tactic in the occult Masonic agenda. For example, the *acacia* plant is a symbol used in the 3rd Degree of Masonry to indicate the notion of life-after-death - and Buck writes on the topic that *"Here, again, we see a symbol ages old, revived and adopted in many forms, and further, that Immortality was not 'brought to light' for the first and only time by the 'Man of Sorrows' of the Christians; yet in every case is the symbol none the less true. Whether any of these sun-gods or Redeemers were historical characters or not, the symbolism teaches every-where the same eternal truths: the Resurrection and the Life; Redemption and Immortality."*

Here, you can plainly see Buck combining the Satanic deceptions of **Perennialism** and **Salvation Without Christ**. In fact, this is almost preaching salvation *period*: life without end, no matter what, simply as a matter of course.

He echoes Hall's lies about Christ being a symbol of the sun...subtly implies that Christ may never have existed at all...then lies once more that salvation through Christ is just the same old "eternal truth."

This begs a question we have not yet asked: *"Why?"* If Jesus were doing no more than preaching the *"same eternal truths"* that all these *"sun-gods or Redeemers"* had in the past, why would He and the Apostles have gone to such great lengths to specifically explain that they were *not* doing that?

Why would St. Paul have spent so much time preaching the Spirit and the superiority of Christian faith over anything in the pagan world, if it were just a new iteration of the same old beliefs?

*Why would the Martyrs of the Christian faith have willingly suffered excruciating torture just to tell the same old story?*

The occult philosophers never even attempt to answer the question, since the answer would undermine the entire deception. Buck then continues by reiterating the same old Kabbalah nonsense you have seen from several authors, writing that *"Beneath the Hebrew text of the Pentateuch lies concealed the science of the Kab[b]alah."*

I spent much time and energy studying religious texts and operating from the assumption that the "secret doctrine" existed. I studied Dion Fortune, I studied the Hermetic Order Of the Golden Dawn, and I believed that I would eventually come across the "key" that unlocked its "mysteries" if I just studied hard enough.

But the more I studied, the more convinced I became that it was all one big lie. Nobody can point to any part of the entire Bible and state, conclusively and persuasively, that it corresponds to anything in the Kabbalah.

All that you discover, upon that path, is one "hint" that leads to another "hint." A letter represents a word, which symbolizes an animal, corresponding to a zodiac sign, signifying a concept which itself leads back to yet another letter.

There is no point or meaning to any of it; occultism is an endless loop of nothing.

In retrospect, it is hard to believe that I once looked up to J.D. Buck as a brilliant philosopher who had struck upon some deep and powerful truth. For example, I once considered the following passage to be a real gem of esoteric wisdom.

*"There is a Grand Science known as Magic, and every real Master is a Magician. Feared by the ignorant, and ridiculed by the 'learned' the Divine Science and its Masters have, nevertheless, existed in all ages, and exist to-day. Masonry in its deeper meaning and recondite mysteries constitutes and possesses this Science, and all genuine Initiation consists in an orderly unfolding of the natural powers of the neophyte, so that he shall become the very thing he desires to possess…Even such the rituals of Masonry have become to many. That the Christ-life and the power that made Jesus to be called Christos, Master, whereby he healed the sick, cast out devils, and foretold future events, is the same Life revealed and attained by initiation in the Greater Mysteries of Antiquity, is perfectly plain."*

Not only is it not "perfectly plain," it is not even feasible. Nobody who has experienced the true power, grace, and majesty of God could consider such nonsense for even a single moment.

Can you hear the arrogance and condescension in Buck's voice, as he subtly belittles those he deems too stupid to understand these "mysteries?"

He continues to assert that everything we think we know about Christ is, in "fact," simply our lack of understanding some deeper Kabbalistic mystery.

*"The Sacred Books of all religions, including those of the Jews and the Christians, were and are no more than*

*parables and allegories of the real Secret Doctrine, transcribed for the ignorant and superstitious masses."*

Ask an occultist what exactly this "Secret Doctrine" is, and he will tell you it "has yet to be fully discovered." Perhaps he will say instead that it "used to be known, but then the Christians destroyed it!"

Whatever his answer will be, it will not actually be an answer. One must study *this* system, then *that* one. He must be initiated in *this* school, and reach *that* level.

Around and around the carousel goes, until his body and mind are home to a legion of demons. These demons then fill the man's mind with the 4 Satanic Deceptions until he has completely lost sight of what it even means to be human.

Buck, having reached a very advanced stage of prelest, eventually decided there was no God but himself. This is still the foundational belief of deluded Satanists all across the world.

After a lifetime of participation in the occult, he concludes that *"Humanity…is the only Personal God; and Christos is the realization, or perfection of this Divine Persona, in Individual conscious experience…It will be urged by modern Theologians that this view dethrones Christ. To this objection the answer is that any other view orphans Humanity. It is far more important that men should strive to become Christs than that they should believe that Jesus was Christ…From the Essenes, the Schools of Alexandria then in all their glory, from the Kab[b]alah and the philosophy of Plato, the Christian mysteries were derived…The Religion of Jesus was in every respect that of the Mysteries."*

As you were taught in **Holy And Unholy Mysteries,** even a cursory look through Christian history proves otherwise.

And as I have already mentioned, the prophet Isaiah talked about this exact phenomenon when he was foretelling the nation's destruction. Recall that he recorded in **Isaiah 47:10, *"Your wisdom and knowledge mislead you when you say to yourself, 'I am, and there is none besides me.'"***

It is one of many passages in the Bible which seek to illustrate the folly of the natural man's reasoning and the limits of what can be understood using logic alone. This is why St. Paul later wrote in **1 Corinthians 2:4** that *"my speech and my preaching was not with enticing words of man's wisdom, but in demonstration of the Spirit and of power."*

Indeed, the failings of reason compared to the truths of the Holy Spirit make up a consistent theme throughout both the Old and New Testaments. This is why it was so important for Pike, before launching into any of his New Age goofiness, to establish doubt as to the credibility of the Orthodox Church and its Holy Fathers in the first place.

It is worth noting that, while Buck's book discusses an enormous variety of religions and philosophical systems, Christianity is the *only* one he ever denigrates.

He doesn't have a single unkind word to say about any other faith, as demons have no reason to insult or dismantle false doctrines in the first place. Their only real opponent is the true Light -- that which Jesus Christ brought into the world and illuminates the hearts and minds of every real believer -- and so it is only this Light which they seek to snuff out with their many and varied lies.

In <u>Mystic Masonry</u>, Buck regularly refers to Christians as "*bigoted sectarians.*" Unlike the more subtle liars we have studied, Buck goes so far as to explicitly say that Masonry and Christianity are philosophical opponents.

With Christianity, he writes that *"...the real genius of Masonry is in perpetual conflict. For [Christians], the universal and unqualified Brotherhood of Man, is a dead letter, for he believes that only himself and his chosen associates can be saved."*

If you are a Christian reading such a statement, how could you still believe that Masonic philosophy is compatible with your faith? One of its greatest proponents has just told you, in clear language, that it is not!

Even more insidious and evil than that, Buck appears to invent a quote from St. Augustine which he believes will help his efforts to dismantle true Christianity.

He does so by pretending that Christianity is "secretly teaching" the exact pagan philosophy which it spends so much time and energy preaching against. Surely, you can see the parallels between Buck's quote about St. Augustine and what Hall said about St. Justin.

Here is the quote Buck uses, which according to my research _does not exist_ outside of occult and theosophical works. Searching for this passage on the world's biggest online search engine doesn't reveal a single actual citation from anything St. Augustine actually wrote.

According to Buck, St. Augustine wrote that *"What is now called the Christian Religion existed among the ancients, and was not absent from the human race until Christ came, from which time the true religion, which existed already, began to be called Christian."*

If this quote does exist in any of St. Augustine's corpus, it would surely be from his days as a Gnostic, which he later retracted upon his conversion to the One, Holy, Catholic and Apostolic Church of Jesus Christ.

Is there anything more wicked and demonic than this, to so utterly insult our Savior as to suggest that He brought nothing new to the world?

Let us pray that all such men receive mercy for their trespasses and forgiveness for their errors. As the heart of the Gospel is compassion and love, we must ever remember that the Devil would like nothing more than for us to hate our enemies (the same way he hates us).

Let us not act in the image of the Devil, therefore, but rather in the image of God. Let us pray for our enemies and bless those who curse us, recalling that even at the Crucifixion our Lord prayed for mercy on his persecutors.

In this manner, the Church's interaction with Freemasonry may be most effective not only for their salvation - but for ours as well. It is not the existence of our enemies that can truly harm us, but rather our own merciless attitude towards them.

So let us pray for the whole world, those within the Church and those without, that all may be healed and come to know the glory of our risen and eternal King.

As you have learned, Freemasonry does not preach orthodox **Theology**, orthodox **Christology**, or an orthodox understanding of either mankind's origins or our ultimate destiny. It should come as no surprise, then, that only a heterodox **Soteriology** could possibly result from such heretical views.

"If you declare with your mouth, 'Jesus is Lord,' and believe in your heart that God raised him from the dead, you will be saved. For it is with your heart that you believe and are justified, and it is with your mouth that you profess your faith and are saved."

Romans 10:9-10

# SOTERIOLOGY

In Orthodox Christianity, the word *salvation* is generally described as the process of becoming more and more like Christ over time - ideally culminating in becoming a Saint upon the death of the physical body. We call this process *theosis*. It cannot be achieved by human effort alone, but requires cooperation with God's free gifts of His uncreated grace and energies.

The vehicle by which we arrive there is improved renunciation of self, and the road on which it travels is moment-to-moment spiritual warfare. Our goal is to improve ourselves not in the worldly sense of becoming smarter, faster, and stronger - but rather in the spiritual sense of becoming humbler, gentler, and kinder.

The *telos* (or endpoint) of Orthodoxy, therefore, can be summarized as improving one's union with Christ through self-denial and asceticism. We are called - and challenged - to imitate Him in every way, progressively breaking our chains to the world through prayer, fasting, vigils, repentance, the sacraments, and worship.

Through this process, we learn to rely less on ourselves and more on God in order to claim victory in the unseen warfare - overcoming that which would otherwise defeat us.

Masonry's soteriology, or theory of salvation, is best summarized by Pike in his commentary on the 32nd Degree, *Sublime Prince Of The Royal Secret*. In it, he writes that *"Freemasonry is the subjugation of the Human that is in man by the Divine; the Conquest of the Appetites and Passions by the Moral Sense and the Reason; a continual effort, struggle, and warfare of the Spiritual against the Material and Sensual. That victory, when it has been achieved and secured, and the conqueror may rest upon his shield and wear the well-earned laurels, is the true Holy Empire. To achieve it, the Mason must first attain a solid conviction, founded upon reason, that he hath within him a spiritual nature, a soul that is not to die when the body is dissolved, but is to continue to exist and to advance toward perfection through all the ages of eternity, and to see more and more clearly, as it draws nearer unto God, the Light of the Divine Presence. This is the Philosophy the Ancient and Accepted Rite teaches him; and it encourages him to persevere by helping him to believe that his free will is entirely consistent with God's Omnipotence and Omniscience; that He is not only infinite in power, and of infinite wisdom, but of infinite mercy, and an infinitely tender pity and love for the frail and imperfect creatures that He has made."*

Of course, there is much a Christian can agree with in this statement. We *do* believe in the conquest of the spiritual over the material, we *do* believe that the soul survives the death of the body, and we *do* believe that man's free will is consistent with God's infinite power.

But we *don't* believe that **Salvation Without Christ** is possible, we *don't* believe that the "appetites and passions" can be circumscribed solely by "the moral sense and the reason," and we *don't* believe that souls which die in a state of sin will later be able to work their way to Heaven.

By preaching a deceptive doctrine of salvation to Jews, Hindus, Muslims and Buddhists, Freemasonry gives false hope to those whose only hope for salvation is Jesus Christ and His Gospel. If they believe they can work their way to Heaven by any other means, they are mistaken - and the consequences could be eternal.

Now, it is not Orthodox to uniformly declare that all outside the Church are automatically condemned. Certainly, there are some outside the visible Church who are leading more virtuous lives than some within it - and only God can decide what to do with them.

But what we *can* say without hesitation is that, though eternal judgment is up to God alone, preaching salvation by any means but Christ is to deliberately mislead those most in need of Him - and this is certainly a deed which God will take into account on that dreadful day of reckoning.

Furthermore, Pike lobs a number of attacks against ascetics and monastics throughout the pages of Morals And Dogma. He seems to have a peculiar disdain for those who truly turn their backs on the world, rather than trying to "fix" it. He writes that *"Masonry does not occupy itself with crying down this world, with its splendid beauty, its thrilling interests, its glorious works, its noble and holy affections; nor exhort us to detach our hearts from the earthly life, as empty, fleeting, and unworthy, and fix them upon Heaven, as the only sphere deserving the love of the loving or the meditation of the wise. It teaches that man has high duties to perform, and a high destiny to fulfill, on this earth."*

He then quotes again from Greg's Creed Of Christendom, asserting that man *"is sent into this world, not to be constantly hankering after, dreaming of, preparing for another; but to do his duty and fulfill his destiny on this earth; to do all that lies in his power to improve it, to render it a scene of elevated happiness to himself, to those around him, to those who are to come after him."*

Greg continues his attacks on such men as the Desert Fathers of Orthodoxy, claiming that *"They take very unprofitable pains, who endeavor to persuade men that they are obliged wholly to despise this world, and all that is in it, even whilst they themselves live here. God hath not taken all that pains in forming and framing and furnishing and adorning the world, that they who were made by Him to live in it should despise it."* Pike comments on this passage by adding that *"It is useless to attempt to extinguish all those affections and passions which are and always will be inseparable from human nature."*

What a nihilistic view of the work Christ can do for us! By quoting Greg's anti-monastic errors, Pike exposes the fruits of his worldview: that despite his encouragement towards morality and self-improvement, he does not genuinely believe that man can overcome his fallen nature to truly become more Christlike.

Pike continues that *"The Unseen cannot hold a higher place in our affections than the Seen and the Familiar. The law of our being is Love of Life, and its interests and adornment; love of the world in which our lot is cast, engrossment with the interests and affections of earth."*

If you are familiar with the Scriptures, then you may already know what St. John the Evangelist taught us regarding the sentiment that Pike is encouraging. St. John teaches in his first Epistle, "**Do not love the world or anything in the world. If anyone loves the world, love for the Father is not in them. For everything in the world - the lust of the flesh, the lust of the eyes, and the pride of life - comes not from the Father but from the world."** **(1 John 2:15-16)** This exhortation is seconded by St. James, who teaches that "**friendship with the world means enmity with God."** **(James 4:4)**

Once more, we see a Masonic teaching strictly at odds with a Biblical one. Pike teaches to enjoy life, to keep your eyes fixed on the earth and the things which they can readily perceive. Orthodoxy teaches death to the world in preparation for life in Heaven.

Just to hammer this point home even more deeply, Pike includes another passage in which Greg states that *"The Mason does not exhort others to an ascetic undervaluing of this life, as an insignificant and unworthy portion of existence; for that demands feelings which are unnatural...and teaches us to look rather to a future life for the compensation of social evils, than to this life for their cure; and so does injury to the cause of virtue and to that of social progress."*

Personally, I do not recall reading about "social progress" in the writings of either the Holy Apostles or the Fathers who followed in their footsteps. I do recall being taught to *"render unto Caesar what is Caesar's"* **(Matthew 22:21)** as well as to *"Submit yourselves for the Lord's sake to every human institution, whether to a king as the one in authority, or to governors as sent by him for the punishment of evildoers and the praise of those who do right."* **(1 Peter 2:13-14)**

I recall being taught that Satan is *"the god of this world"* **(2 Corinthians 4:4)** and *"Do not put your trust in princes and kings, who cannot save."* **(Psalms 146:3)**

St. Seraphim of Sarov wrote that *"Fear of God is acquired when a man, renouncing the world and everything that is in the world, concentrates all his thoughts and feelings on the single thought of God's law, and immerses himself entirely in contemplation of God and in a feeling of the blessedness promised to the Saints."*

In a similar vein, St. Gregory Palamas wrote that *"To know God truly in so far as this is possible is incomparably superior to the philosophy of the Greeks, and similarly to know what place man has in relation to God surpasses all their wisdom."*

The Orthodox Fathers all agreed that asceticism was a holy path to God. But a clear picture emerges that, in the eyes of Freemasonry, a life of ascetic self-denial is not a way to follow God - but rather, an unnatural waste of man's earthly potential. While some Protestants may agree with such anti-monastic sentiments, most Roman Catholics and Eastern Orthodox Christians better understand the command to "***be not conformed to this world.***" **(Romans 12:2)**

Christ commands us to fix our eyes on eternal life with God and to leave salvation in His hands; Pike commands us to fix our eyes on society and do everything in our power to cure its ills.

Each man must decide for himself which command to follow.

Therefore, the telos of Freemasonry is not *theosis* at all. Whereas Orthodoxy teaches union with God by *renouncing* oneself and the world, Masonry teaches that a man should focus on *improving* them instead.

To that end, the fraternity introduces a particular set of symbols to new candidates in their very first Degree - symbols which will remain metaphors for the journey throughout his entire Masonic career.

Drawing from the language and tools of architectural stonemasonry, each candidate is shown what are called the "rough and perfect ashlars" many times in the fraternity. They are, essentially, two stones which might potentially be used in the building of a structure - one is rough and jagged, the other perfect and smooth.

As per the metaphor, each new Mason is taught that, as he stands upon entering the fraternity, he is a "rough ashlar:" he has the potential to become a useful and well-fitting stone in the building of Freemasonry, but first all of his rough edges and imperfections must be smoothed out by the practice of Masonic values. Thus, a Mason's goal is to go from the "rough" to the "perfect" ashlar in regards to his mind, character, and sense of duty.

While I don't have any particular problem with that metaphor, as it can be spiritually applied to any Christian man as well, the issue is that a building made of many-faithed ashlars will be inherently unstable.

Further, the well-known Mason J.S.M Ward wrote that Masonry *"has taught that each man can, by himself, work out his own conception of God and thereby achieve salvation."*

This is the opposite of what Christians believe, and is simply a newer (and religiously-indifferent) form of the condemned heresy of *Pelagianism*. The quote from Ward demonstrates, once again and in yet another form, that Masonry places zero value on the revealed Word or will of God. It elevates reason to the level of revelation, inherently neglecting man's limited and sinful state of being.

I mentioned earlier that the Lodge forbids any discussion of religion and politics within its closed meetings. Thus, the superstructure of Freemasonry can only stand strong when its members suppress their own spiritual and religious truths.

In the opening paragraphs of his commentary on the 8th Degree, *Intendant Of The Building*, Pike writes that *"Step by step men must advance toward Perfection; and each Masonic Degree is meant to be one of those steps."*

Such is the explanation of the rough and perfect ashlars.

## On Immortality

It turns out that both Masons and Christians pursue immortality...but in very different ways. While Christians seek eternal glory in the presence of God, Masons seek - in Pike's words - *"That our influences shall survive us, and be living forces when we are in our graves; and not merely that our names shall be remembered; but rather that our words shall be read, our acts spoken of, our names recollected and mentioned when we are dead, as evidence that those influences live and rule, sway and control some portion of mankind and the world - this is the aspiration of the human soul."*

What Pike does not clarify, of course, is that this is the aspiration of the *fallen* human soul. To seek fame, to seek influence, to seek power, to seek the recognition of one's own name is strictly opposed to the aspiration of our *true* nature - which is to seek nothing but union and communion with our Creator.

These things may occur, of course - and they do, with the Lives of the Saints and the lessons they've left behind - but always as a result of humility and self-denial, and never as a result of their desire for fame or influence. Whatever good has been said of the Saints has been said by those who loved them, and never by the Saints themselves.

How does a Mason achieve the endpoint of Masonry? Pike writes in the opening paragraphs of his commentary on the *Secret Master* Degree that "*You are [o]n the path that leads up the slope of the mountain of Truth; and it depends upon your secrecy, obedience, and fidelity, whether you will advance or remain stationary.*"

Not a word about holiness, not a word about renunciation of the self. Simply obedience to the fraternity and keeping its teachings secret. I do not know what "Truth" that leads to, but I am fairly certain that I am better off without it.

Pike clarifies further that "*To be immortal in our influences projected far into the slow-approaching Future, makes life most worthy and most glorious.*"

John Dewey, quoted many times by Pike, agrees with this sentiment in writing that "*Earth, which binds many in chains, is to the Mason both the starting-place and the goal of immortality. Many it buries in the rubbish of dull cares and wearying vanities; but to the Mason it is the lofty mount of meditation, where Heaven, and Infinity and Eternity are spread before him and around him."*

Thus, even immortality itself means something completely different to a genuine Christian than it does to such high-ranking Masons. To a Christian, immortality means enjoying the presence of God eternally in the age to come. To a Mason, it means keeping one's name in the minds of men on earth.

This is not only foreign to Christian thinking; it is the polar opposite of the humility and self-denial to which we are called. To a Christian, the aspiration for fame and influence is a passion against which to fight - not a healthy desire in which to indulge.

The Masonic inability to distinguish between Heaven and the present age are indicative, more than anything else, of a lack of true Christian faith and grace. The notion that the world was created good, but fell into ruin due to human disobedience, is foreign to Dewey and Pike's ways of thinking.

And yet, this is exactly what both the Scriptures and the Fathers invariably teach. Christ and His earliest disciples taught us that this world is passing away, to be replaced by a renewed and deified cosmos. They further taught that we should set our minds on resurrection in the age to come, rather than trying to make a permanent utopia out of that which is fundamentally temporary.

Not only does Masonry openly preach worldly recognition and **Salvation Without Christ**, but some have even complained that a Mason might think he needs anything on top of Masonry to be saved at all.

In his <u>Textbook Of Masonic Jurisprudence</u>, Albert Mackey whines that *"Within a few years an attempt has been made by some Grand Lodges to add to these simple moral and religious qualifications another, which requires a belief in the divine authenticity of the Scriptures. It is much to be regretted that Masons will sometimes forget the fundamental law of their institution, and endeavor to add or detract from the perfect integrity of the building as it was left them by their predecessors. Whenever this is done, the beauty of our temple must suffer. Thus, in the instance here referred to, the fundamental law of Masonry requires only a belief in the Supreme Architect of the universe, and in a future life, while it says with peculiar toleration, that in all matters of religious belief Masons are only expected to be of that religion in which all men agree. Under the shelter of this wise provision, the Christian and the Jews, the Mohammedan and the Brahmin are permitted to unite around a common altar, and Masonry becomes in practice, as well as in theory, universal."*

Clearly, some Christians even within the Lodge recognized that something was missing by neglecting the name and work of Jesus Christ, and actively took steps to ameliorate the situation. Mackey responded by bemoaning such an injury to Masonry's *"fundamental law"* and *"beauty."*

We have now covered all of the theological ground which I set out to explore in <u>On The Masons And Their Lies</u>. As you have now examined and judged every facet of the tree of Freemasonry, let us move onto the fruit which it bears.

More specifically, it is now time to reveal the Christian world's responses to Freemasonry and the ideals it promotes.

"The roots of modern apostasy lay in scientific atheism, dialectical materialism, rationalism, illuminism, laicism, and Freemasonry; which is the mother of them all."

Pope Pius XXII

# MASONRY AND THE CHURCHES

Pike once complained that *"A people content with the thoughts made for them by the priests of a church will be content with Royalty by Divine Right - the Church and the Throne mutually sustaining each other. They will smother schism and reap infidelity and indifference; and while the battle for freedom goes on around them, they will only sink the more apathetically into servitude and a deep trance."*

Given his attitude and all that you have learned thus far, it should be easy to understand why Freemasonry has butted heads with Christianity over time - in any and every place where the two have come into contact. That is why, in the final chapter of our journey on this topic, I have compiled several statements from various Christian groups on Masonry and its compatibility with their teachings (or lack thereof).

This section exists as a quick go-to reference guide for priests and pastors dealing with the Masonic spirit in their parishes and among their members. It will also be useful, of course, for Christian Freemasons to see what their own Churches have had to say about the institution.

Sometimes, Freemasonry is mentioned by name in the letters and statements which I have been able to find. Other times, it is simply included under the larger umbrella of the *"secret societies"* warned against by a particular church.

According to the essay <u>Freemasonry And The Christian</u> by Eddy D. Field II and Eddy D. Field III, *"An overwhelming number of Christian denominations have condemned Freemasonry, including the Roman Catholic Church, the*

Methodist Church of England, the Wesleyan Methodist Church, the Russian Orthodox Church, the Synod Anglican Church of England, the Assemblies of God, the Church of the Nazarene, the Orthodox Presbyterian Church, the Reformed Presbyterian Church, the Christian Reformed Church in America, the Evangelical Mennonite Church, the Church of Scotland, the Free Church of Scotland, General Association of Regular Baptist Churches, Grace Brethren, Independent Fundamentalist Churches of America, the Evangelical Lutheran Synod, the Baptist Union of Scotland, The Lutheran Church-Missouri Synod, the Wisconsin Evangelical Lutheran Synod, and the Presbyterian Church in America."*

As you read through this section, a useful question to ask yourself is: *"What is more likely - that Masonry is a religion at odds with Christianity, or that every single Christian group which has studied the topic at length is wrong?"*

We will begin with the Roman Catholics, who have been embroiled in a public war against Freemasonry for nearly 300 years - and made many statements on the topic.

## Roman Catholicism

In 1738 - just 21 years after Freemasonry went public with the United Grand Lodge of England - the Roman Catholic Church undertook a very serious investigation into Italian Freemasonry and related "secret societies." At the conclusion of the investigation, Pope Clement XII decreed the first canonical prohibition of Masonic association in the Papal bull *In Eminenti Apostolatus*.

After summarizing Masonry's secretive nature, the Pope wrote that *"Therefore, bearing in mind the great harm which is often caused by such Societies or Conventicles not only to the peace of the temporal state but also to the well-being of *souls, and realizing that they do not hold by either civil or canonical sanctions; and since We are taught by the divine word that it is the part of the faithful servant and of the master of the Lord's household to watch day and night lest such men as these break into the household like thieves, and like foxes seek to destroy the vineyard; in fact, to prevent the hearts of the simple being perverted, and the innocent secretly wounded by their arrows, and to block that broad road which could be opened to the uncorrected commission of sin and for the other just and reasonable motives known to Us; We therefore, having taken counsel of some of Our Venerable Brothers among the Cardinals of the Holy Roman Church, and also of Our own accord and with certain knowledge and mature deliberations, with the plenitude of the Apostolic power do hereby determine and have decreed that these same Societies, Companies, Assemblies, Meetings, Congregations, or Conventicles of Liberi Muratori or Francs Massons, or whatever other name they may go by, are to be condemned and prohibited, and by Our present Constitution, valid for ever, We do condemn and prohibit them.*

*Wherefore We command most strictly and in virtue of holy obedience, all the faithful of whatever state, grade, condition, order, dignity or pre-eminence, whether clerical or lay, secular or regular, even those who are entitled to specific and individual mention, that none, under any pretext or for any reason, shall dare or presume to enter, propagate or support these aforesaid societies of Liberi Muratori or Francs Massons, or however else they are called, or to receive them in their houses or dwellings or to hide them, be enrolled among them, joined to them, be present with them, give power or permission for them to meet elsewhere, to help them in any way, to give them in any way advice, encouragement or support either openly or in secret, directly or indirectly, on their own or through others; nor are they to urge others or tell them, incite or persuade them to be enrolled in such societies or to be counted among their number, or to be present or to assist them in any way; but they must stay completely clear of such Societies, Companies, Assemblies, Meetings, Congregations or Conventicles, under pain of excommunication for all the above mentioned people, which is incurred by the very deed without any declaration being required, and from which no one can obtain the benefit of absolution, other than at the hour of death, except through Ourselves or the Roman Pontiff of the time."*

According to Wikipedia, *"The ban in In eminenti apostolatus was reiterated and expanded upon by Benedict XIV (1751), Pius VII (1821), Leo XII (1825), Pius VIII (1829), Gregory XVI (1832), and Pius IX (1846, 1849, 1864, 1865, 1869, 1873)."*

The ban continued to be upheld over time, and Canon 2335 (written in 1917) declared that *"Those who enlist in Masonic sects or other associations of the same kind, which plot against the Church or against lawful civil authority, ipso facto incur the excommunication simply reserved to the Apostolic See."*

Wikipedia further states that *"In 1980, after six years of dialogue with representatives of the United Grand Lodges of Germany and investigation of Masonic rituals, the DBK produced a report on Freemasonry listing twelve conclusions. Among the DBK's conclusions were that Freemasonry denies revelation, and objective truth. They also alleged that religious indifference is fundamental to Freemasonry, and that Freemasonry is Deist, and that it denies the possibility of divine revelation, so threatening the respect due to the Church's teaching office. The sacramental character of Masonic rituals was seen as signifying an individual transformation, offering an alternative path to perfection and having a total claim on the life of a member. It concludes by stating that all lodges are forbidden to Catholics, including Catholic-friendly lodges."*

When the Plenary Congregation of the Pontifical Commission for the Revision of the Code of Canon Law met to discuss Canon 2335 in 1981, the issue at hand was whether to renew the earlier ban on Freemasonry. Cardinal Pietro Palazzini, who wanted the ban to remain in place, stated that *"Freemasonry is more dangerous than Communism, because while Communism is the explicit enemy of the Church, Freemasonry is more subtle."*

Alas, the majority of Cardinals voted to eliminate the ban, and the punishment of automatic excommunication was lifted. In its place, the 1983 Congregation For The Doctrine Of The Faith formalized a new *Declaration On Masonic Associations*.

Somewhat of a departure from the earlier excommunication rule, the new canon nonetheless imposes a strict penalty. Under the new rule, any Roman Catholic who participates in Freemasonry is considered to be *"in a grave state of sin and may not receive Holy Communion...the Church's negative judgment in regard to Masonic association(s) remains unchanged since their principles have always been considered irreconcilable with the doctrine of the Church and therefore membership in them remains forbidden."*

This decision is still in effect today.

Though the penalty has therefore changed from automatic excommunication to simply being barred from the sacraments and the normal life of the Roman Catholic Church, the official stance has never changed: Roman Catholicism and Freemasonry are not compatible.

If you are an active Roman Catholic and also a Mason, you have been violating your own Church's official doctrine every time you've participated in the sacraments. You have a choice to make...and I encourage you to choose wisely.

## Protestantism

For this section, I will speak only of two major Protestant groups which, despite being heterodox themselves, nevertheless confess an orthodox view of the Holy Trinity. I have chosen these specific examples because I feel their conclusions encompass and explain the majority of Protestant objections to Freemasonry.

Extra-heterodox and non-Trinitarian groups like the Jehovah's Witnesses and the Mormons will not be mentioned, especially because Mormonism was founded by a Freemason - and that particular discussion is simply outside the scope of the present work.

The Lutheran Church-Missouri Synod declared that *"'The Lodge' in this evaluation has reference to secret societies and organizations that include religious themes, teachings and practices in their initiation rites, regular meeting activities, and funeral rituals. Freemasonry serves as a primary example of such an organization that espouses and promotes teachings and practices that conflict with the fundamental teachings of the Christian faith. The concerns raised concerning Freemasonry apply also - though usually to a lesser degree - to other lodge organizations such as the Moose, Eagles, Elks, and Oddfellows, along with the women's and youth auxiliaries of these lodges, particularly those associated with the Masonic lodge.*

*One of the Landmarks of Freemasonry is the belief in the existence of a Supreme Being. However, the Supreme Being of Freemasonry is officially a generic god designed by intent to be universally acceptable to all who would seek admittance to the Masonic lodge. This god is a unitarian, not trinitarian, Supreme Being.*

*According to Freemasonry man is not totally sinful, just imperfect. In the first degree of Masonry the perfectibility of man is taught with reference to rough and smooth ashlars, stones that have been hewn by hand and made square. The rituals state: 'By the Rough Ashlar we are reminded of our rude and imperfect state by nature; by the Perfect Ashlar, of that state of perfection at which we hope to arrive by a virtuous education, by our own endeavors, and by the blessing of God.' Freemasonry's view of human nature parallels closely the modern New Age view that man is in some sense divine and has the capacity to become his own god.*

*The Scriptures teach that Christians with integrity are to confess Christ and His Gospel boldly and without compromise...[and that] He has revealed Himself to us in His Word (John 17; Matt. 10:32; Rom. 10:9-10; 1 Tim. 6:12;1 John 2:23, etc.). In the view of this evaluation, it is a compromise of the Christian confession to take part in ritual, religious acts, in the name of a generic deity, that intentionally delete the Name of the true God and Jesus Christ whom God has sent to be the only Savior of the world (Luke 12:8)."*

The Orthodox Presbyterian Church came to precisely the same conclusions in 1942. In their <u>Report Of The Committee On Secret Societies</u>, their Ninth General Assembly wrote that *"The committee finds that the evidence presented concerning the religion of Masonry permits but one conclusion. Although a number of the objections commonly brought against Masonry seem to the committee not to be weighty, yet it is driven to the conclusion that Masonry is a religious institution and as such is definitely anti-Christian.*

*Far be it from the committee to assert that there are no Christians among the members of the Masonic fraternity. Just as a great many who trust for eternal life solely in the merits of Christ continue as members of churches that have denied the faith, so undoubtedly many sincere Christians, uninformed, or even misinformed, concerning the true character of Freemasonry, hold membership in it without compunction of conscience. But that in no way alters the fact that membership in the Masonic fraternity is inconsistent with Christianity. There is no room for any reasonable doubt as to Masonry's being a religion. Not only do the symbols, rites and temples of this order point unmistakably to it as a religion, but a great many Masonic authors of note emphatically declare it to be just that. Of almost numberless quotations that could be given here the committee has selected a few.*

*J.S.M. Ward, the author of several standard Masonic works, defines religion as 'a system of teaching moral truth associated with a belief in God' and then declares: 'I consider Freemasonry is a sufficiently organized school of mysticism to be entitled to be called a religion.' He goes on to say: 'I boldly aver that Freemasonry is a religion, yet in no way conflicts with any other religion, unless that religion holds that no one outside its portals can be saved' (Freemasonry: Its Aims and Ideals, pp. 182, 185, 187).*

*T. S. Webb says in his Masonic Monitor: 'The meeting of a Masonic Lodge is strictly a religious ceremony. The religious tenets of Masonry are few, simple, but fundamental. No lodge or Masonic assembly can be regularly opened or closed without prayer' (p. 284).*

*Albert G. Mackey, General High Priest of the General Grand Chapter of the United States, and the author of numerous works on Masonry, has this to say: 'Freemasonry is emphatically a religious institution; it teaches the existence of God. It points to the celestial canopy above where is the Eternal Lodge and where He presides. It instructs us in the way to reach the portals of that distant temple' (The Mystic*

*Tie, p. 32). And in his Lexicon of Freemasonry the same celebrated authority asserts: 'The religion, then, of Masonry is pure Theism" (p. 404).'*

*Extremely significant is the testimony of Joseph Fort Newton, a zealous advocate of Masonic principles. He deplores the fact that within the lodge there are many who regard it as 'a mere social order inculcating ethical ideals and practicing philanthropy.' He continues: 'As some of us prefer to put it, Masonry is not a religion but Religion - not a church but a worship, in which men of all religions may unite' (The Religion of Masonry, pp. 10, 11).*

*With this agrees A. G. Mackey's declaration: 'The truth is that Masonry is undoubtedly a religious institution, its religion being of that universal kind in which all men agree' (Textbook of Masonic Jurisdiction, p. 95). To be sure, H. L. Haywood says that 'there is no such thing as a Masonic philosophy, just as there is no such thing as a Masonic religion' (The Great Teachings of Masonry, p. 18).*

*But on careful analysis it becomes clear that he means that Masonry is not to be put in a class with other religions; in a word, that it is a super-religion. For he asserts that Masonry has a religious foundation all its own and that its religion is universal (Idem, p. 99). No doubt, Haywood would agree with Newton that 'Masonry is not a religion, but Religion.'*

*Such is the unmistakable testimony, not of critics of Masonry, but of Masonic authors who are recognized by Masonry itself as authorities. Either Masonry as a religion is in agreement with Christianity, or it must be at odds with Christianity. Either it is Christian, or it must be anti-Christian."*

As you can see, these groups came to the very same conclusions as I did when I wrote this book.

# Orthodox Christianity

Let us now look at what various Orthodox Christian communions have said on the topic of Freemasonry. We have had at least one Ecumenical Patriarch, Meletius IV of Constantinople, who was an acknowledged Freemason in a Greek Lodge.

As mentioned to me by an Orthodox priest at the very beginning of this project, the Antiochian archdiocese has said nothing one way or the other - and I would very much like for this book to get into the hands of whoever in their Patriarchate is in a position to make such a statement. They have laity joining the Freemasons simply because a quick search reveals no warnings *not* to, and that's a fairly easy situation to remedy for those with the power and the will to do so.

On its official website, the Orthodox Church of America unambiguously declares that *"It is forbidden for an Orthodox Christian to be a member of the Masonic Fraternity because many of its teachings stand in direct conflict with those of Orthodox Christianity."*

The Archbishop of Cyrus in 1815, Cyprianus, made the same point - but far more graphically. In <u>The Aphorism Against Freemasonry</u>, he wrote that *"Wherefore, clad in the sacred vestments of epitrachelion and omophorion we say, 'If any man preach unto you any other gospel than that which we have preached unto you, even though an angel from heaven, let him be accursed.' (Gal. 1,8,9) As many as are befitting, that pursue after such a diabolic and lawless employment of Freemasonry, and all they that follow unto their infatuation and unto their error, let them be excommunicated and accursed by the Father, the Son, and the Holy Spirit. After death, they shall be unpardoned, indissoluble, and bloated. Groaning and trembling, as Cain, shall they be upon the earth. (Gen. 4:14). The earth shall cleave and swallow them up, as Dathan and Abiram (Num. 16, 31-32). The wrath of God shall be upon their heads, and their portion together with Judas the betrayer. An angel of the Lord will prosecute them with a flaming sword and, unto their life's termination, they will not know of progress. Let their works and toil be unblessed and let them become a cloud of dust, as of a summer threshing floor. And all they indeed that shall abide still unto their wickedness will have such a recompense. But as many as shall go out from the midst of them and shall be separated, and having spat out their abominable heresy, and shall go afar off from their accursed infatuation, such kind shall receive the wages of the zealot Phineas; rather let them be blessed and forgiven by the Father, and the Son, and the Holy Spirit, the Only unconfused and undivided Trinity, the One God in nature, and by us His servants."*

The Bishops of the Church of Greece also convened in 1933 to study the Lodge as a group. After careful examination, they concluded that *"Freemasonry is not simply a philanthropic union or a philosophical school, but constitutes a mystagogical system which reminds us of the ancient heathen mystery-religions and cults from which it descends, and is their continuation and regeneration...Such a link between Freemasonry and the ancient idolatrous mysteries is also manifested by all that is enacted and performed at the initiations...Thus Freemasonry is, as granted, a mystery-religion, quite different, separate, and alien to the Christian faith."*

The Russian Orthodox Church Outside Russia insists on excommunication for Masonic affiliation. In 1932, the ROCOR Council of Bishops wrote to the Faithful that *"Freemasonry is a secret international organisation to struggle with God, Christianity, and all National Governments, and especially Christian Governments. In the international organization the first place of influence and importance belongs to the Jewish membership. Because of this, and other important reasons, it is forbidden for all Orthodox Christians to become Freemasons.*

*In view of what has been stated above, the Holy Council decides to: (1) Condemn Masonry as a doctrine and an organization contrary to Christianity. (2) Condemn equally all the doctrines and organizations having an affinity with Masonry, like Theosophy, Anthroposophy, all forms of "Christian gnosticism" [which would include such things as "Christian Yoga," "Christian Zen," etc], and the YMCA. (3) Recommend to the diocesan bishops and to chiefs of missions to furnish their clergy with all information which may serve to enlighten the faithful regarding the above-mentioned erroneous doctrines and organizations. (4) Recommend to pastors the necessity of questioning every person presenting himself for confession with a view to finding out whether or not that person is a member of a Masonic organization and whether or not he shares its doctrines. If it appears that the person is a member or shares its teaching, explain to him that participation in these organizations is incompatible with the name of Christian, with being a member of the Church of Christ. That he must take a firm decision to break with Masonry and with doctrines related to it; and if he does not do so, not to admit him to Holy Communion; and if he should refuse to repent, to excommunicate him from the Holy Church."*

Despite their differences, many of the various Christian groups in the world today share the exact same perspective on the Masonic fraternity: it is against their creed, it is a religion unto itself, and its members are in spiritual danger by joining or associating with it.

Therefore, let no man delude himself into thinking he can be a faithful Christian and a faithful Mason at the same time. They are mutually exclusive, and he ultimately must choose either one system or the other.

"Therefore, brethren, stand fast, and hold the traditions which you have been taught, whether by word of mouth or epistle."

2 Thessalonians 2:15

# CONCLUSION

Dearly beloved in Christ, I have now taught you everything I have to teach on the subject of Freemasonry. I hope that, through these efforts, you can easily recognize that the teachings of the fraternity are incompatible with the Gospel of Jesus Christ.

Ironically, you now know more about Freemasonry than most of its members do.

As I told you in the beginning, I have said nothing new. I am simply one in a long line of apologists who have laid bare the traps of the Enemy for a new generation to see.

While I hope this exposé has sufficiently revealed the inherent problems with the Masonic institution, I wish to communicate once more that my intention is *not* to condemn.

It is not Christian to consider the members themselves evil; rather, let us consider them to be victims of forces far beyond the strength of God-less men to resist. Like you and I, they are created in the image of God...and like you and I, they are led astray by their own desires.

The position they are in, as members of the fraternity, is no different than how you or I behave when we are not in communion with Jesus Christ.

We are all tempted by our adversary, and without God on our side we have no chance of victory. For as the great Lorenzo Scupoli writes in Spiritual Combat, *"If you rely on yourself, you will not be able to resist even the slightest attack of the Enemy."*

We mortals are fragile and gullible creatures, easy prey for demons unless properly prepared for battle. In Freemasonry, the Enemy's attacks lead man to a misleading, distorted, and dangerous view of salvation.

Instead of becoming one with Jesus Christ, who is God Himself and the fullness of all perfection, Masonic adepts are instead taught to "reascend on the astral planes" in order to lead more successful lives.

The Kabbalah is used as the model and basis for man's "ascent," which takes places by way of thinly-veiled ceremonial magic and being "initiated into higher Grades."

Having been on both sides of the "Mystery initiation" fence, it is my personal opinion that what is taught as "initiation" is, in reality, minor possession by demonic forces. "Higher Grades," or Degrees in the Masonic system, mean nothing more or less than a greater degree of possession - by which the person gradually becomes more and more of a puppet or vessel for the various dark forces being invoked.

By the time a man or woman reaches the highest level of these modern Mystery Schools, he or she has become completely one with Satan; there is no more room in the mind or soul for the will of God. At that point, the person is utterly enslaved; they are subjected to beings far more powerful than they, and cannot break their chains except by the power of Jesus Christ.

What presents itself as holy and philosophical is, in reality, a guaranteed way to lose your soul. People who take that path often wind up with broken minds as well, gradually becoming more insane the more deeply they get involved.

If you bought this book to help someone you know, it is important to understand the condition in which you are approaching them - and it should be understood as one of powerless subservience to forces beyond their comprehension.

They are not bad people, they are not consciously choosing evil, and they have fallen for one of the most elaborate deceptions in the history of Satan's war with mankind.

That is why I wish to end this book with St. Paul's exhortation on spiritual warfare, as written in **Ephesians 6:11-17.**

*"Put on the full armor of God, so that you can take your stand against the devil's schemes. For our struggle is not against flesh and blood, but against the rulers, against the authorities, against the powers of this dark world and against the spiritual forces of evil in the heavenly realms. Therefore put on the full armor of God, so that when the day of evil comes, you may be able to stand your ground, and after you have done everything, to stand. Stand firm then, with the belt of truth buckled around your waist, with the breastplate of righteousness in place, and with your feet fitted with the readiness that comes from the gospel of peace. In addition to all this, take up the shield of faith, with which you can extinguish all the flaming arrows of the evil one. Take the helmet of salvation and the sword of the Spirit, which is the word of God."*

May God bless you, have mercy on you, and grant you life eternal. *In the name of the Father, and the Son, and the Holy Spirit. Amen.*

# ABOUT THE AUTHOR

Since leaving Freemasonry, Michael has devoted his free time to educating other Christians on occult and esoteric topics.

He is also the CEO of **Level Up Copy And Consulting**, a digital marketing agency based in Southern California.

Made in the USA
Monee, IL
15 August 2021